Theodore Roosevelt

The President Who Changed America's Look at Nature

(How Two Maine Woodsmen Taught the Future President to Survive)

Andrew Veale

Published By **Jordan Levy**

Andrew Veale

Theodore Roosevelt: The President Who Changed America's Look at Nature (How Two Maine Woodsmen Taught the Future President to Survive)

ISBN 978-1-7753142-9-5

No part of this guidebook shall be reproduced in any form without permission in writing from the publisher except in the case of brief quotations embodied in critical articles or reviews.

Legal & Disclaimer

The information contained in this book is not designed to replace or take the place of any form of medicine or professional medical advice. The information in this book has been provided for educational & entertainment purposes only.

The information contained in this book has been compiled from sources deemed reliable, and it is accurate to the best of the Author's knowledge; however, the Author cannot guarantee its accuracy and validity and cannot be held liable for any errors or omissions. Changes are periodically made to this book. You must consult your doctor or get professional medical advice before using any of the suggested remedies, techniques, or information in this book.

Upon using the information contained in this book, you agree to hold harmless the Author from and against any damages, costs, and expenses, including any legal fees potentially resulting from the application of any of the information provided by this guide. This disclaimer applies to any damages or injury caused by the use and application, whether directly or indirectly, of any advice or information presented, whether for breach of contract, tort, negligence, personal injury, criminal intent, or under any other cause of action.

You agree to accept all risks of using the information presented inside this book. You need to consult a professional medical practitioner in order to ensure you are both able and healthy enough to participate in this program.

Table Of Contents

Chapter 1: Life In Brief

Theodore Roosevelt, who came into place of work in 1901 and served till 1909, is taken into consideration the primary contemporary-day President due to the truth he appreciably extended the have an impact on and electricity of the government workplace. From the Civil War to the flip of the twentieth century, the seat of energy in the countrywide government resided within the U.S. Congress. Beginning inside the Eighteen 1980s, the govt branch regularly stepped forward its strength. Roosevelt seized in this style, believing that the President had the proper to use all powers except people who had been specially denied him to carry out his dreams. As a cease result, the President, in place of Congress or the political occasions, have become the middle of the American political region. As President, Roosevelt challenged the thoughts of restricted government and individualism. In their stead, he endorsed government regulation to acquire social and financial justice. He used govt orders to carry out his desires, specifically in conservation, and waged an competitive distant places coverage. He have end up also a really well-known President and the primary to apply the media to attraction right away to the humans, bypassing the political events and profession politicians.

Early Life

Frail and sickly as a boy, "Teedie" Roosevelt superior a rugged body as a teenager and became a lifelong suggest of exercise and the "strenuous existence." After graduating from Harvard, Roosevelt married Alice Hathaway Lee and studied law at Columbia University. He dropped out after a 12 months to pursue politics, triumphing a seat in the New York Assembly in 1882.

A double tragedy struck Roosevelt in 1884, at the same time as his mother and his spouse died inside the identical residence on the same day. Roosevelt spent years out West in an attempt to get better, tending cows as a rancher and busting outlaws as a frontier sheriff. In 1886, he back to New York and married his childhood sweetheart, Edith Kermit Carow. They raised six children, together with Roosevelt's daughter from his first marriage. After losing a campaign for mayor, he served as Civil Service commissioner, president of the New York City Police Board, and assistant secretary of the Navy. All the on the same time as, he tested honesty in workplace, frightening the birthday celebration bosses who anticipated him to disregard the law in want of partisan politics.

War Hero and Vice President

When the Spanish-American War broke out in 1898, Roosevelt volunteered as commander of the first U.S. Volunteer Cavalry, called the Rough Riders, essential a bold price on San Juan Hill. Returning as a battle hero, he have grow to be governor of New York and started out to showcase an independence that disillusioned the country's political device. To stop Roosevelt's reforms, party bosses "kicked him upstairs" to the vice presidency beneath William McKinley, believing that during this role he may be now not able to keep his innovative guidelines. Roosevelt campaigned vigorously for McKinley in 1900—one commentator remarked, "Tis Teddy by myself this is on foot, an' he ain't a runnin', he's a gallopin'." Roosevelt's efforts helped make sure victory for McKinley. But his time as vice chairman turn out to be short; McKinley modified into assassinated in 1901, making Roosevelt the President of america.

By the 1904 election, Roosevelt changed into eager to be elected President in his very personal proper. To attain this, he knew that he had to art work with Republican Party leaders. He promised to keep lower back on additives of his innovative time desk in alternate for a unfastened hand in overseas affairs. He additionally had been given the reluctant guide of rich capitalists, who feared his cutting-edge measures, but feared a Democratic victory even greater. TR received in a landslide, turning into the primary President to be elected after gaining office due to the lack of existence of his predecessor. Upon victory, he vowed now not to run for some other time period in 1908, a promise he got here to remorse.

Modern Presidency

As President, Roosevelt worked to make certain that the authorities superior the lives of American residents. His "Square Deal" domestic application pondered the innovative name to reform the American workplace, starting up welfare law and government law of business corporation. He grow to be furthermore the country's first environmentalist President, setting apart nearly two hundred million acres for country wide forests, reserves, and natural world refuges. In remote places coverage, Roosevelt preferred to make the us a international power by using developing its impact global. He led the try to steady rights to assemble the Panama Canal, one of the excellent engineering feats at that point. He moreover issued his "corollary" to the Monroe Doctrine, which set up the United States due to the fact the "policeman" of the Western Hemisphere. In addition, he used his function as President to help negotiate peace agreements between belligerent international locations, believing that the location have to settle global disputes through global family members as opposed to conflict. Roosevelt is taken into consideration the primary modern-day-day U.S. President because of the truth he extensively strengthened the energy of the government branch. He have become furthermore an incredibly popular President—so well-known after leaving place of work in 1909 that he grow to be able to mount a vital run for the presidency another time in 1912. Believing that his successor, William Howard Taft, had did now not maintain his software of reform, TR threw his hat into the ring as a candidate for the Progressive Party. Although Roosevelt became defeated by using Democrat Woodrow Wilson, his efforts resulted in the advent of one of the maximum large 1/3 events in U.S. Records. With the onset of World War I in 1914, Roosevelt endorsed that the US prepare itself for struggle. Accordingly, he have become in particular important of Wilson's pledge of neutrality. Once america entered the warfare in 1917, all 4 of Roosevelt's sons volunteered to serve, which substantially pleased the former President. The death of his youngest son, Quentin, left him deeply distraught. Theodore Roosevelt died a whole lot much less than a yr later.

LIFE BEFORE THE PRESIDENCY

Theodore Roosevelt have turn out to be born on October 27, 1858, and grew up in New York City, the second of four youngsters. His father, Theodore, Sr., modified right right into a properly-to-do businessman and philanthropist. His mom, Martha "Mittie" Roosevelt, became a Southerner, raised on a plantation in Georgia. "Teedie" grew up surrounded through the love of his parents and siblings. But he changed into generally a sickly little one with allergic reactions. As a teen, he determined that he need to "make his frame," and he undertook a software of gymnastics and weight-lifting, which helped him broaden a rugged body. Thereafter, Roosevelt have turn out to be a lifelong endorse of exercise and the "strenuous lifestyles." He continuously observed time for bodily difficult paintings together with hiking, using horses, and swimming. As a younger boy, Roosevelt turned into tutored at home with the aid of the usage of manner of personal teachers. He traveled broadly via Europe and the Middle East alongside with his own family at a few degree in the past due 1860s and early 1870s, once residing with a gaggle family in Germany for 5 months. In 1876, he entered Harvard College, wherein he studied lots of topics, along with German, natural history, zoology, forensics, and composition. He additionally persisted his physical endeavors, taking up boxing and wrestling as new pastimes.

During college, Roosevelt fell in love with Alice Hathaway Lee, a more youthful female from a distinguished New England banking own family he met via a chum at Harvard. They had been married in October 1880. Roosevelt then enrolled in Columbia Law School, however dropped out after three hundred and sixty five days to start a profession in public service. He changed into elected to the New York Assembly and served terms from 1882 to 1884. A double tragedy struck Roosevelt in 1884. On

February twelfth, Alice gave starting to a daughter, Alice Lee. Two days later, Roosevelt's mother died of typhoid fever and his partner died of kidney disease inner some hours of every extraordinary—and in the same residence. For the subsequent few months, a devastated Roosevelt threw himself into political art work to break out his grief. Finally, he left his daughter in the care of his sister and fled to the Dakota Badlands. Once out West, Roosevelt soaked inside the frontier way of life. He supplied two ranches and 1000 head of livestock. He flourished in the hardships of the western frontier, the usage of for days, looking grizzly bears, herding cows as a rancher, and chasing outlaws as a frontier sheriff. Roosevelt headed once more East in 1886; a devastating iciness the subsequent 365 days worn out most of his cattle. Although he can also frequent the Dakota Badlands in subsequent years to seek, he became ready depart the West and move lower back to his former life. One of the motives he did so have become because of a rediscovered love together alongside together with his adolescence sweetheart, Edith Kermit Carow. The were married in England in 1886 and moved to Oyster Bay, New York, into a house referred to as Sagamore Hill. In addition to elevating Roosevelt's first infant, Alice, he and Edith had five children: Theodore, Kermit, Ethel, Archibald, and Quentin.

Renewed Political Spirit

After returning to New York, Roosevelt persevered his writing profession, which commenced out with the e-book of his e-book, The Naval War of 1812, in 1882. He wrote some of books in the course of this period, which include The Life of Thomas Hart Benton (1887), The Life of Gouverneur Morris (1888), and The Winning of the West (4 volumes, 1889-1896). Roosevelt furthermore resumed his political career with the useful resource of taking walks unsuccessfully for mayor of New York City in

1886. In 1888, he campaigned for Republican presidential nominee Benjamin Harrison. When Harrison obtained the election, he appointed Roosevelt to the U.S. Civil Service Commission. Roosevelt have become re-appointed to the Commission with the resource of Democratic President Grover Cleveland in 1893. As commissioner, he worked difficult to put into effect the civil employer prison recommendations, notwithstanding the truth that he regularly clashed with party regulars and politicians who wanted him to brush aside the law in preference of patronage. Roosevelt served dutifully as a commissioner until he customary the presidency of the New York City Police Board in 1895. He showed honesty in place of work, masses to the displeasure of celebration bosses. He moreover wiped clean up the corrupt Police Board and strictly enforced legal guidelines banning the sale of liquor on the Sabbath.

In 1897, the newly elected Republican President, William McKinley, appointed Roosevelt assistant secretary of the Navy. Roosevelt had prolonged believed inside the importance of the Navy and the feature it finished in countrywide safety. As acting secretary of the Navy, he answered to the explosion of the U.S. Battleship Maine in Havana Harbor in 1898 by way of putting the Navy on entire alert. Roosevelt informed Commodore George Dewey to make prepared for war with Spain by taking the vital steps for bottling up the Spanish squadron in Asian waters. He additionally asked Dewey to prepare for the probably invasion of the Philippines.

The Rough Riders

When the Spanish-American War started out out out, Roosevelt resigned as assistant secretary of the Navy and volunteered for provider as commander the number one U.S. Volunteer Cavalry, a unit referred to as the Rough Riders—an elite commercial employer organisation comprised of Ivy League gents, western cowboys, sheriffs, prospectors, cops, and Native Americans. Once in Cuba, Roosevelt extremely good himself with the resource of main them on a price—on foot—up San Juan Hill (genuinely Kettle Hill) at the outskirts of Santiago. The contingent suffered heavy casualties. The Rough Riders again to the united states as battle heroes. Their numerous backgrounds, colorful chief, and bravado on the battlefield brought them huge hobby. Roosevelt in my opinion reveled in his time inside the army. He later wrote about his army exploits: "I should as a substitute have led that charge and earned my colonelcy than served 3 terms in the United States Senate. It makes me enjoy as regardless of the fact that I ought to now leave a few thing to my kids so you can feature an apology for my having existed."

Governor

Roosevelt back domestic a conflict hero and fixed the eye of Republican leaders in New York who had been searching out a gubernatorial candidate. He agreed to run for governor in competition to a famous Democrat, Judge Augustus van Wyck, the candidate of Tammany Hall. Roosevelt carried the election thru only a few thousand votes; his victory stemmed in massive part from the paintings of the usa's Republican Party boss, Thomas C. Platt, who threw the general help of his political system within the returned of the hero of San Juan Hill. Although Platt and Roosevelt had agreed to are looking for advice from each exceptional on matters of insurance and patronage, the present day governor become his very very own guy. TR steadfastly refused to lease birthday party regulars as State Insurance Commissioner or Public Works Commissioner—the 2 most essential patronage jobs inside the state. When Governor Roosevelt supported a invoice for the taxation of the price and belongings of public offerings (gas, water, electric powered, and streetcars), his moves caused an explosive ruin with Platt. Almost in a unmarried day the coverage groups, the improvement contractors, and the privately owned public company businesses realized that all the cash they have been contributing to Platt's political device brought them little if any affect with Governor Roosevelt.

Boss Platt knew that something needed to be completed with the governor before he in reality destroyed the Republican u . S . System. Consulting with Mark Hanna, the top Republican political boss inside the country, Platt conspired to "kick [Roosevelt] upstairs" to the vice presidency in 1900. (Vice President Garret Hobart had just died in workplace.) This may hold Roosevelt from on foot for a 2nd term in New York (the governorship modified right into a -yr time period in the ones days). Roosevelt reluctantly agreed, persuaded that the vice presidency should probable bring about a shot on the White House in 1904. He furthermore knew that the birthday celebration bosses had rigged the convention, making it almost not possible for him to avoid being nominated.

1900 Vice Presidential Campaign

The Republican conference nominated TR via acclamation. Thereafter, Roosevelt campaigned furiously for the Republican presidential candidate, William McKinley, matching his Democratic combatants, William Jennings Bryan and Adlai E. Stevenson, flow into for go with the flow. Roosevelt traveled extra than 21,000 miles on a unique advertising advertising marketing campaign train, making hundreds of speeches, and similarly than 3 million human beings observed him in person. He spoke in 567 cities in twenty-four states. "Tis Tiddy by myself that is walking," determined Mr. Dooley (a press columnist who used an exaggerated Irish accent to make political observations) "an' he ain't a runnin', he is gallopin'." The Republican charge tag beaten the Democrats, racking up an 861,757 vote plurality, the biggest Republican victory in years. McKinley gained the well-known vote of seven.2 million (292 Electoral College votes) to Bryan's 6.Three million (155 Electoral College votes). McKinley received his bid for reelection over Bryan thru an exceptional huge margin than he had garnered in 1896.

In September 1901, however, an murderer's bullet killed President McKinley. This tragedy placed Theodore Roosevelt ("that damned cowboy"—constant with Mark Hanna, the top Republican political boss inside the state) within the White House as america's twenty-sixth President. He have end up the youngest character ever to serve in that capability. Neither the dominion nor the presidency may ever be the equal yet again.

Chapter 2: Campaigns And Elections

The Campaign and Election of 1904:

After Roosevelt acceded to the presidency in 1901, he speedy started to consider the way to win election as President in his very own proper. He observed out that in spite of the reality that he did now not typically accept as real with conservative Republicans in Congress, he wished their assist to be able to win the nomination in 1904. To that stop, he worked out an information with legislators, in particular Senator Nelson W. Aldrich of Rhode Island, which gave him a unfastened hand in overseas affairs in return for containing once more the extra contemporary devices of his domestic time desk. But TR did now not refrain from using the government place of work to interrupt up monopolies, at the side of the Northern Securities Company, to mediate in exertions disputes among unions and management, as he did within the coal miners' strike in 1902, and to apply the White House as a "bully pulpit," from which he lectured the dominion on how authorities need to alter large corporation. Fearful that his anti-organisation sentiments had soured birthday celebration bosses, Roosevelt toned down his rhetoric in 1903. Most importantly, he modified into able to region his human beings in key birthday celebration positions and maneuvered Mark Hanna, now the Chairman of the Republican National Committee, to indicate his candidacy several months previous to the 1904 conference. Then TR have turn out to be to the public, preserving press conferences, launching a national tour of western states that lasted for thirty days, and boldly issuing an authorities order that provided pensions for all veterans some of the a long term of sixty-two and sixty-seven.

With Mark Hanna's untimely loss of life previous to the Republican convention in Chicago, really considered one of Roosevelt's primary opposition modified into long beyond, making TR's nomination a foregone end. He have turn out to be nominated unanimously on the first ballot . He picked Senator Charles W. Fairbanks of Indiana—a conservative Republican with near ties to the railroad corporation—as his walking mate. When the Democrats met in St. Louis, they picked conservatives, Judge Alton B. Parker, from New York, and eighty-one-year-antique Henry G. Davis, a rich ex-senator from Virginia and the oldest guy to ever run for the vice-presidency. The Democrats, showcasing themselves due to the fact the "sane and secure choice," attacked the Roosevelt control as "spasmodic, erratic, sensational, extremely good, and arbitrary." Republicans touted Roosevelt's record in overseas coverage and promised more of the identical. Neither Roosevelt nor Parker actively campaigned for the presidency, as changed into the custom.

Over the summer season of 1904, Roosevelt directed the marketing campaign from his the the the front porch at Oyster Bay, issuing lofty statements to his supporters and instructions on approach to Republican us of a parties. Roosevelt obtained a massive sum of money for the advertising marketing campaign from rich capitalists, which embody Edward H. Harriman (the railroad wealthy character), Henry C. Frick (the metal baron), and J.P. Morgan (the monetary potentate of Wall Street). The rich capitalists and their friends contributed extra than $2 million to Roosevelt's marketing and advertising and marketing campaign. They supported Roosevelt because of the reality they favored an "unpredictable head of a predictable birthday celebration" in strength than the "predictable head of an unpredictable birthday party." They could probable have desired Parker as a person, however the Democrats have been truely too populist of their constituency and possibly too radical of their thoughts for the conservative enterprise leaders ever to consider.

The election, however, had in no way been uncertain. TR won 336 electoral votes to Parker's one hundred forty. He took every america of the us outdoor of the South, which include Missouri. Roosevelt grow to be immensely well-known and rode to a 2d time period on a large wave of public useful resource, in assessment to three element the dominion had ever visible. After the victory, Roosevelt vowed no longer to run all over again for the presidency, believing it come to be smart to look at the precedent of best serving terms in place of business. However, he got here to regret that promise earlier of the 1908 election, believing he although had a number of his time table to perform. However, he held genuine to his pledge and supported his chosen successor, William Howard Taft, in 1908.

The Campaign and Election of 1912

Before he left place of business in 1909, Roosevelt hand-picked William Howard Taft as his successor and worked to get him elected. Taft had served inside the Roosevelt management as governor of the Philippines and secretary of warfare. During the election, Taft vowed to run the united states absolutely as Roosevelt had. But the today's control modified into off to a rocky start with the outgoing President. After reputedly indicating that he might hold maximum of the existing cabinet people, Taft fast positioned that he is probably better served through his private hand-picked secretaries. Roosevelt have become miffed at having his cupboard members dismissed and at not being consulted on the contemporary appointments.

After Taft's inauguration, Roosevelt traveled in Africa and Europe for extra than a 3 hundred and sixty 5 days. He went on safari alongside together with his son Kermit, wherein he received greater than 3,000 animal trophies, together with 8 elephants, seven hippos, 9 lions, and thirteen rhinos. He then met up with Edith in Egypt, and the two of them journeyed at some stage in Europe, encountering ordinary desires to satisfy and greet royalty and politicians. When the Roosevelts once more to New York in June 1910, they have been greeted with the aid of the use of considered considered one of the biggest mass receptions ever given in New York City.

When he first arrived decrease lower back inside the United States, Roosevelt remained noncommittal at the Taft presidency. He desired time to evaluate Taft's average performance earlier than making any judgments. However, some of his antique buddies had already delivered him bad critiques. Gifford Pinchot became so irritated with Taft regarding conservation that he had earlier traveled to Italy to meet Roosevelt and communicate the state of affairs. Once TR decrease again domestic, he changed into frequently visited with the resource of using antique buddies who decried Taft's intended efforts to undo his artwork.

During this period, progressivism became often growing from the local and u . S . A . Stage to the national degree. Increasing numbers of people at a few degree in the united states of america supported growing the position of the federal authorities to ensure the welfare of the people. Pressured by using the present day wing of the Republican Party to task Taft in 1912, Roosevelt weighed his options. Eventually he determined to throw "his hat into the hoop" and run towards his former protégé.

The Republicans met in Chicago in June 1912, hopelessly split among the Roosevelt progressives and the supporters of President Taft. Roosevelt came to the convention having received a chain of preferential primaries that placed him earlier of the President within the race for party delegates. Taft, but, controlled the conference ground, and his backers managed to exclude maximum of the Roosevelt delegates by using no longer spotting their credentials. These approaches enraged TR, who then refused to allow himself to be nominated, paving the manner for Taft to win on the primary poll.

Roosevelt and his supporters abandoned the G.O.P. And reconvened in Chicago weeks later to form the Progressive Party. They then nominated TR as their presidential candidate with Governor Hiram Johnson of California as his walking mate. Roosevelt electrified the conference with a dramatic speech wherein he announced that "we stand at Armageddon, and we conflict for the Lord." Declaring that he felt "as strong as a Bull Moose," Roosevelt gave the present day celebration its well-known name—the Bull Moose Party—and defined its celebration platform as "New Nationalism." Its tenets blanketed political justice and economic opportunity, and it sought a minimum profits for women; an eight-hour workday; a social protection gadget; a rustic good sized fitness issuer; a federal securities charge; and direct election of U.S. Senators. The platform additionally supported the initiative, referendum, and keep in mind as technique for the people to exert greater direct manage over authorities. TR worried approximately the electricity of the minority—frequently politicians—over the bulk and idea the ones changes should make government greater accountable to the people.

The Democrats nominated the reform governor of New Jersey, Woodrow Wilson, for President and Thomas R. Marshall, the governor of Indiana, as vice president. Wilson's platform, referred to as "New Freedom," known as for limits on marketing campaign contributions thru companies, tariff reductions, new and more potent antitrust laws, banking and foreign exchange reform, a federal profits tax, direct election of senators, and a single-term presidency. Although Roosevelt and Wilson were every progressives, they differed over the approach and quantity to which government have to intrude or adjust the states and the monetary system.

Differences between New Nationalism and New Freedom over trusts and the tariff have come to be a important trouble of the campaign. Roosevelt believed the federal authorities need to act as a "trustee" for the American humans, controlling and supervising the economic machine within the public hobby. Wilson had extra reservations about a massive federal authorities and sought a pass lower back to a more decentralized republic. He argued that if massive enterprise business agency had been deprived of artificial benefits, together with the protecting tariff and monopolies, the natural forces of competition might guarantee anyone an equal danger at achievement—therefore minimizing the placement of government. Whereas Roosevelt differentiated among "excellent" and "terrible" trusts, Wilson recommended that each one monopolies have been unstable to the dominion. Roosevelt's colourful man or woman helped him conquer the drawback of strolling as a 3rd-birthday party candidate, and he and Wilson contended fiercely for the help of citizens inquisitive about reform. Near the give up of the advertising advertising campaign, TR dramatized his energy through insisting on completing a marketing campaign speech no matter an assailant's bullet lodged in his chest. Fortunately, the bullet had been bogged down by means of the usage of the pages of a thick speech he had in his coat pocket, but Roosevelt's courageous—in all likelihood foolhardy—act reminded Americans of what they cherished about him.

Wilson captured forty one.Nine percent of the vote to Roosevelt's 27.Four percentage and Taft's 23.1 percentage. Socialist Party candidate Eugene Debs acquired 6 percent of the vote. Despite the divided well-known vote, Wilson compiled 435 electoral votes in contrast to Roosevelt's 88 and Taft's eight. Roosevelt received in six states—California, Michigan, Minnesota, Pennsylvania, South Dakota, and Washington. Despite its loss, the sturdy showing of the Progressive Party signaled the emergence of a full-size force in U.S. Political history. It additionally reflected a growing progressive spirit in the United States. Together with Wilson and Debs, Roosevelt had challenged the conservative wing of the Republican Party and left it discredited. In addition, irrespective of the fact that TR misplaced the election, a number of his New Nationalism software software modified into enacted sooner or later of Wilson's presidency.

Chapter 3: Domestic Affairs

When Theodore Roosevelt took the oath of workplace in September 1901, he presided over a rustic that had changed extensively in modern-day a few years. The population of america had nearly doubled from 1870 to 1900 as immigrants came to U.S. Cities to paintings in the united states's burgeoning factories. As the united states have end up increasingly city and enterprise, it obtained a few of the attributes common to business international locations—overcrowded cities, horrible operating conditions, excellent monetary disparity, and the political dominance of huge commercial enterprise. At the flip of the 20th century, Americans had all started out to search for methods to address a number of the ones troubles. As chief government, Roosevelt felt empowered thru the usage of the people to assist make sure social justice and financial opportunity thru government law. He turned into not an intensive, however; TR believed that massive commercial enterprise business enterprise grow to be a herbal part of a maturing monetary device and, therefore, determined no purpose to abolish it. He in no way endorsed essentially changing American society or the monetary system to deal with numerous economic and social ills. In fact, he frequently said that there have to be reform that lets in you to stave off socialism; if authorities did not act, the human beings should flip to extra excessive measures to are searching out treatments. In addition, TR turn out to be a baby-kisser who understood the want to compromise that allows you to region into impact his ideas. Coming into workplace following William McKinley's assassination, Roosevelt pledged to preserve the fallen President's policies so as no longer to upset the country in a time of mourning. And even though he started to chart his private route, Roosevelt knew that he needed to art work with congressional Republicans to get the G.O.P. Nomination for President in 1904.

The Great Regulator

One of Roosevelt's important ideals changed into that the government had the proper to adjust big organisation to guard the welfare of society. However, this concept turned into as a substitute untested. Although Congress had exceeded the Sherman Antitrust Act in 1890, former Presidents had handiest used it sparingly. So even as the Department of Justice filed in form in early 1902 towards the Northern Securities Company, it despatched shockwaves through the agency community. The wholesome alarmed the economic business business enterprise network, which had was hoping that Roosevelt may additionally comply with precedent and maintain a "arms-off" method to the market financial machine. At hassle have become the claim that the Northern Securities Company—a huge railroad combination created by means of the use of the usage of a syndicate of wealthy industrialists and financiers led through J. P. Morgan—violated the Sherman Antitrust Act as it have become a monopoly. In 1904, the U.S. Supreme Court dominated in choose of the government and ordered the corporation dismantled. The excessive courtroom docket's motion was a major victory for the management and put the agency network on phrase that although this come to be a Republican control, it might now not provide business business enterprise free rein to function with out regard for the overall public welfare.

Roosevelt then have become his attention to the kingdom's railroads, in detail because of the truth the Interstate Commerce Commission (ICC) had notified the control approximately abuses in the enterprise. In addition, a huge section of the populace supported efforts to alter the railroads due to the truth such a whole lot of humans and groups were counting on them. Roosevelt's first fulfillment on this location was the

Elkins Act of 1903, which ended the exercising of railroad groups granting delivery rebates to positive companies. The rebates allowed huge organizations to deliver items for an lousy lot lower costs than smaller corporations should acquire. However, the railroads and large groups had been able to undermine the act. Recognizing that the Elkins Act emerge as no longer powerful, Roosevelt pursued in addition railroad law and undertook simply one among his best home reform efforts. The regulation, that have turn out to be referred to as the Hepburn Act, proposed enhancing the powers of the Interstate Commerce Commission to consist of the capacity to regulate transport costs on railroads. One of the primary sticking points of the invoice was what role the courts may play in reviewing the expenses. Conservative senators who unfavorable the law, appearing on behalf of the railroad agency, tried to use judicial assessment to make the ICC essentially powerless. By giving the courts, which have been considered best to the railroads, the proper to rule on man or woman instances, the ICC had tons much much less electricity to treatment the inequities of the expenses. When Roosevelt encountered this resistance in Congress, he took his case to the human beings, developing a right away attraction on a talking excursion thru the West. He succeeded in pressuring the Senate to approve the regulation. The Hepburn Act marked one of the first instances a President appealed at once to the humans, using the press to help him make his case. The passage of the act have turn out to be considered a top victory for Roosevelt and highlighted his capability to stability competing hobbies to acquire his dreams.

Square Deal

Roosevelt believed that the authorities want to apply its belongings to assist attain financial and social justice. When the usa of a faced an anthracite coal shortage in the fall of 1902 due to a strike in Pennsylvania, the President notion he must intervene. As winter approached and heating shortages had been coming near close to, he started out to formulate thoughts approximately how he should use the authorities administrative center to play a function—regardless of the fact that he did no longer have any legitimate authority to negotiate an give up to the strike. Roosevelt called every the mine proprietors and the representatives of tough paintings collectively on the White House. When control refused to barter, he hatched a plan to pressure the two facets to speak: instead of sending federal troops to interrupt the strike and strain the miners decrease back to paintings, TR threatened to use troops to seize the mines and run them as a federal operation. Faced with Roosevelt's plan, the proprietors and tough paintings unions agreed to post their instances to a price and abide thru its pointers. Roosevelt known as the agreement of the coal strike a "rectangular deal," inferring that everybody won pretty from the settlement. That term soon have emerge as synonymous with Roosevelt's domestic software. The Square Deal worked to stability competing hobbies to create a honest deal for all aspects: difficult artwork and control, client and company, developer and conservationist. TR recognized that his application changed into no longer flawlessly impartial due to the fact the authorities had to intervene greater actively on behalf of the general public to make certain monetary opportunity for all. Roosevelt modified into the primary President to name his domestic software program and the workout short have end up common, with Woodrow Wilson's New Freedom, Franklin D. Roosevelt's New Deal, and Harry S. Truman's Fair Deal.

Conservation

Roosevelt come to be the us of a's first conservationist President. Everywhere he went, he preached the need to keep woodlands and mountain stages as places of shelter and retreat. He identified the American man or woman with the u . S . A .'s barren location regions, believing that our western and frontier historic beyond had shaped American values, behavior, and way of life. The President desired the us to exchange from exploiting herbal assets to carefully dealing with them. He labored with Gifford Pinchot, head of the Forestry Bureau, and Frederick Newell, head of the Reclamation Service, to revolutionize this region of the U.S. Authorities. In 1902, Roosevelt signed the Newlands Reclamation Bill, which used coins from federal land income to gather reservoirs and irrigation works to promote agriculture inside the arid West. After he won reelection in his very very personal right in 1904, Roosevelt felt greater empowered to make vast changes on this location. Working with Pinchot, he moved the Forest Service from the Department of the Interior to the

Department of Agriculture. This gave the Forest Service, and Pinchot as head of it, more electricity to gain its desires. Together, Roosevelt and Pinchot decreased the position of u . S . And network government in the manage of natural property, a coverage that met with huge resistance. Only the federal government, they argued, had the assets to supervise those efforts. Roosevelt used his presidential authority to trouble authorities orders to create 100 and fifty new national forests, growing the amount of blanketed land from 40 million acres to 172 million acres. The President furthermore created five country wide parks, eighteen national monuments, and 51 flowers and fauna refuges.

Roosevelt and the Muckrakers

The emergence of a mass-motion impartial press at during the flip of the century modified the character of print media within the United States. Instead of partisan guides that touted a party line, the countrywide media grow to be turning into extra independent and more likely to expose scandals and abuses. This technology marked the begin of investigative journalism, and the newshounds who led the try were referred to as "muckrakers," a term first used by Roosevelt in a 1906 speech. One of the extraordinary examples of Roosevelt's courting with the muckrakers came after he look at Upton Sinclair's The Jungle, which defined in lurid element the filthy situations in the meat packing industry—wherein rats, putrid meat, and poisoned rat bait had been robotically floor up into sausages. Roosevelt answered via way of the usage of pushing for the Meat Inspection Act and the Pure Food and Drug Act of 1906. Both portions of policies endeared him to the overall public and to those corporations that desired government regulation as a way of attaining countrywide customer requirements.

Roosevelt have become the primary President to apply the energy of the media to attraction right now to the American human beings. He understood that his forceful character, his rambunctious own family, and his many opinions made suitable reproduction for the press. He moreover knew that the media became a first rate way for him to acquire out to the humans, bypassing political occasions and political machines. He used the media as a "bully pulpit" to steer public opinion.

On Race and Civil Rights

Theodore Roosevelt contemplated the racial attitudes of his time, and his domestic record on race and civil rights became a combined bag. He did little to hold black suffrage in the South as those states an increasing number of disenfranchised blacks. He believed that African Americans as a race had been not so correct as whites, but he concept many black humans had been advanced to white humans and must have the ability to reveal their benefit. He brought on a excessive controversy early in his presidency even as he invited Booker T. Washington to dine with him at the White House in October 1901. Roosevelt desired to talk to Washington approximately patronage appointments within the South, and he changed into amazed thru the vilification he obtained in the Southern press; he did no longer express regret for his actions. Although he appointed blacks to a few patronage positions within the South, he have become normally unwilling to combat the political battles essential to win their appointment. One incident particularly taints Roosevelt's popularity on racial problems. In 1906, a small institution of black squaddies become accused of happening a taking photos spree in Brownsville, Texas, killing one white guy and wounding any other.

Chapter 4: Foreign Affairs

Theodore Roosevelt inherited an empire-in-the-making even as he assumed workplace in 1901. After the Spanish-American War in 1898, Spain ceded the Philippines, Puerto Rico, and Guam to the USA. In addition, the usa installation a protectorate over Cuba and annexed Hawaii. For the primary time in its data, the usa had obtained an foreign places empire. As President, Roosevelt favored to increase the affect and status of america on the area degree and make the usa a worldwide strength. He moreover believed that the exportation of American values and ideals may have an ennobling effect on the world. TR's diplomatic maxim turned into to "communicate softly and deliver a large stick," and he maintained that a major government ought to be inclined to use pressure at the equal time as critical while operating towards the paintings of persuasion. He therefore sought to gather a effective and reliable protection for the United States to keep away from conflicts with enemies who may also prey on prone factor. Roosevelt discovered McKinley in finishing the relative isolationism that had dominated the usa for the reason that mid-1800s, performing aggressively in foreign affairs, often with out the help or consent of Congress.

Philippines

One of the situations that Roosevelt inherited upon taking administrative center changed into governance of the Philippines, an island nation in Asia. During the Spanish-American War, the us had taken manage of the archipelago from Spain. When Roosevelt appointed William Howard Taft due to the reality the number one civilian governor of the islands in 1901, Taft recommended the arrival of a civil government with an elected legislative assembly. The Taft management have emerge as able to negotiate with Congress for a bill that blanketed a governor famous, an independent judiciary, and the legislative assembly.

Panama Canal

The maximum top notch of Roosevelt's foreign places insurance obligations grow to be the established order of the Panama Canal. For years, U.S. Naval leaders had dreamed of constructing a passage a few of the Atlantic and Pacific oceans thru Central America. During the struggle with Spain, American ships within the Pacific needed to steam at some point of the pinnacle of South America in -month voyages to join up inside the U.S. Fleet off the coast of Cuba. In 1901, america negotiated with Britain for the aid of an American-controlled canal that is probably built each in Nicaragua or through a strip of land—Panama—owned thru Colombia. In a flourish of closed-door maneuvers, the Senate accredited a route through Panama, contingent upon Colombian approval. When Colombia balked on the phrases of the agreement, the us supported a Panamanian revolution with coins and a naval blockade, the latter of which averted Colombian troops from touchdown in Panama. In 1903, the Hay-Bunau-Varilla Treaty with Panama gave america perpetual control of the canal for a rate of $10 million and an annual charge of $250,000.

When he visited Panama in 1906 to observe the building of the canal, Roosevelt have become the primary U.S. President to go away america all through his time period of administrative center. He favored to see the spectacle, that have turn out to be referred to as one of the worldwide's best engineering feats. Nearly 30,000 employees worked ten-hour days for ten years to build the $4 hundred-million canal, at some stage in which generation American officials have been able to counteract the scourge of Yellow Fever that had ravaged big numbers of canal humans. The Panama Canal turn out to be eventually finished in 1914; through 1925, greater than 5,000 issuer employer ships had traversed the 40 miles of locks every three hundred and sixty 5 days. Once operational, it shortened the voyage from San Francisco to New York with the aid of extra than 8,000 miles. The manner of constructing the canal generated advances in U.S. Era and engineering skills. This challenge moreover transformed the Panama Canal Zone into a high staging place for American navy forces, making the US the dominant navy energy in Central America.

Roosevelt Corollary

Latin America ate up a sincere amount of Roosevelt's time and strength in the course of his first term as President. Venezuela have come to be a focal point of his attention in 1902 while Germany and Britain despatched ships to blockade that u . S . A .'s shoreline. The European international places had given loans to Venezuela that the Venezuelan dictator refused to repay. Although every Germany and Britain assured the Americans that they did not have any territorial designs on Venezuela,

Roosevelt felt aggrieved with the useful aid of their moves and demanded that they comply with arbitration to clear up the dispute. Santo Domingo (now the Dominican Republic) furthermore encountered issues with European global locations. Again, European buyers had appealed to their governments to build up cash from a debt-ridden united states of america Latin American usa. After the Dominican government appealed to the united states, Roosevelt ordered an American collector to assume manage of the customs homes and gather obligations to keep away from possible European army motion.

During the Santo Domingo catastrophe, Roosevelt formulated what became known as the Roosevelt Corollary to the Monroe Doctrine. The Monroe Doctrine, issued in 1823, said that the usa would not acquire European intervention inside the Americas. Roosevelt determined out that if global places inside the Western Hemisphere persevered to have persistent problems, in conjunction with the shortage of capacity to repay foreign places debt, they will emerge as targets of European invention. To preempt such movement and to hold local balance, the President drafted his corollary: the usa have to intrude in any Latin American u.S.A. That manifested intense economic problems. The corollary introduced that the USA might feature the "policeman" of the Western Hemisphere, a insurance which in the end created masses resentment in Latin America.

Peacemaker

Though regularly identified for the aggressiveness of his distant places insurance, Roosevelt grow to be furthermore a peacemaker. His maximum a fulfillment effort at bringing belligerent powers to the negotiating desk concerned a catastrophe that had damaged out in East Asia. Fighting had erupted among Russia and Japan in 1904, following Japan's assault on the Russian fleet at Port Arthur. As the Russo-Japanese War raged on with many Japanese victories, Roosevelt approached every global places approximately mediating peace negotiations. The President longed for a global wherein global places could turn to arbitration rather than war to settle international disputes, and he presented his offerings to this give up. Although Russia and Japan to start with refused his offer, they in the long run conventional his "proper workplaces" to assist negotiate a peace, meeting with Roosevelt in 1905 in Portsmouth, New Hampshire. For his function as mediator, Roosevelt obtained the Nobel Prize for Peace, the first U.S. President to reap this. Roosevelt additionally arbitrated a dispute among France and Germany over the department of Morocco. Britain had recognized French manipulate over Morocco in pass back for French recognition of British manipulate in Egypt. Germany felt excluded through using this settlement and challenged France's role in Morocco. Although the French had a prone claim to Morocco, america couldn't reject it with out rejecting Britain's declare as well. The agreement in 1906 reached at Algeciras, Spain, saved face for Germany but gave France undisputed manage over Morocco; it moreover paved the manner for British control over Egypt. Some historians assume that Roosevelt's intervention in those heat spots avoided preventing that could have engulfed all of Europe and Asia in a international war. In any case, Roosevelt's actions notably strengthened Anglo-French ties with the US.

Great White Fleet

Roosevelt believed that a large and effective Navy changed into an important problem of countrywide defense because it served as a sturdy deterrent to America's enemies. During his tenure as President, he constructed the U.S. Navy into one in all the largest in the worldwide, through convincing Congress to add battleships to the fleet and developing its quantity of enlisted guys. In 1907, he proposed sending the fleet out on a international excursion. His motives have been many: to expose off the "Great White Fleet" and impress particular worldwide locations round the location with U.S. Naval strength; to allow the Navy to gain the experience of worldwide tour; and to drum up home resource for his naval software. In December 1907, a fleet of 16 battleships left Hampton Roads, Virginia, and traveled round the world, returning domestic fourteen months later in February 1909.

Chapter 5: Life After The Presidency

After dropping the 1912 election to Woodrow Wilson, Roosevelt and his son Kermit launched right into a voyage into the jungles of Brazil to discover the River of Doubt inside the Amazon region. During the seven-month, 15,000-mile expedition, Roosevelt contacted malaria and suffered a excessive contamination after injuring his leg in a supply accident. Following his circulate once more to the USA, he spent his days writing scientific essays and data books. When World War I broke out in Europe, the previous President led the reason for military preparedness, happy that the country want to be part of the war try. He became substantially upset in President Wilson's call for neutrality and denounced his united states of america's state of being inactive. When the usa in the end entered the struggle in 1917, he furnished to installation a volunteer branch but the War Department grew to emerge as him down. However, all four of his sons volunteered to combat in the war. When his youngest son, Quentin, changed into shot down and killed on the same time as flying a task in Germany, Roosevelt have become despondent. Thereafter, notwithstanding the reality that he persevered to tour the kingdom making speeches in pick of struggle bonds and the war, his mood and voice were much less enthusiastic. For the first time in his life, sadness overtook the as quickly as unconquerable warrior. Theodore Roosevelt died in his sleep on January 6, 1919, in his desired residence at Sagamore Hill in Oyster Bay, New York. One commentator said that lack of existence needed to take him at the same time as he slept else it might have had a fight on its fingers.

FAMILY LIFE

The nation had by no means stated a own family in the White House quite just like the Roosevelts. The public loved to comply with the adventures of the Roosevelt extended family; the President understood that his own family changed right right into a political asset and made it available, to 3 diploma, to the media. When Roosevelt married Edith Kermit Carow in 1886, he already had a daughter, Alice, from his first marriage. He and Edith had 5 more kids— Theodore, Kermit, Edith, Archibald, and Quentin.

For TR, his circle of relatives changed into like having his personal personal circus. His kids have been anywhere, having the whole run of the region. They took their desired pony, Algonquin, into the White House elevator, worried touring officers with a 4-foot King snake, and dropped water balloons at the heads of White House guards. The grand romp persisted at the summer time White House, Sagamore Hill, the family's home in Oyster Bay, New York. There, the President led the kids and clearly all people who passed off to be visiting on hours-long impediment hikes, picnics, and swims within the ocean. Roosevelt furthermore loved to interact family, friends, and site site visitors in grand tale-telling commands about ghosts and the cowboys whom Roosevelt had diagnosed out West. He taught the men to area and the girls to run. He in no way held all over again in his affections or in his praise for braveness and aggressiveness. He nearly drove his spouse, Edith, to distraction along together with his antics, and he or she regularly knowledgeable her wonderful buddies that the President have become virtually an ornery little boy at coronary coronary heart.

THE AMERICAN FRANCHISE

The country's population numbered 76 million humans in 1900. Eight years later, via way of the surrender of Roosevelt's 2nd time period, it had multiplied to 88 million. At the equal time, the usa was becoming an metropolis country, with wider segments of the populace becoming a member of the personnel. The percent that lived on farms had declined from 60 to fifty 4 percentage, whilst the amount of ladies maintaining down jobs elevated, rising from 18 to 21 percentage of the entire exertions stress. More and greater of these jogging ladies were married—25 percentage of all women operating in 1910 as compared to 15 percent in 1900. The high-quality new u . S . To go into the Union in the course of the Roosevelt years become Oklahoma (1907).

Limiting the Franchise

Several essential procedural adjustments within the American franchise happened in the direction of the Roosevelt years. First, the Progressive Movement undermined vintage birthday celebration systems and as a result critically reduced standard voter participation in elections. Angry that conventional partisanship had ended in political workplaces being staffed through "boodlers," crooks, and party hacks, progressives supported reforms aimed in the route of destroying the energy of party bosses. Such measures because of the fact the direct primary, the initiative, the referendum, the do not forget, and the direct election of senators were aimed closer to returning energy to an knowledgeable and accountable electorate unaffected by using the use of manner of party machines or boss politics.

Second, the range of registered citizens fell significantly in cities and towns wherein immigrants dominated the population. Nearly each united states of america in the Union handed non-public registration laws among 1890 and 1920, which required identity certificates and private appearances at wonderful authorities workplaces. Most laws required residency for a high pleasant period of time previous to registration, similarly to among registration and voting. These prison pointers reduced the participation of walking people who did not join up because of artwork schedules or, in the case of new immigrants, have been intimidated by means of manner of manner of the complicated guidelines written in English. Some states, together with New York, required that the ones registering display literacy within the English language, a barrier many immigrants couldn't triumph over.

Numerous states that had allowed non-citizens to vote inside the nineteenth century reversed themselves within the 20th. By 1920, simplest seven states despite the truth that allowed non-residents to vote—and people have been states with few immigrants. The newly normal Bureau of Immigration and Naturalization (1906), furthermore, notably multiplied the boundaries to citizenship. Applicants were forced to seem earlier than a decide (located thru using witnesses to vouch for his or her ethical character and right citizenship) who tested them in English on American records and civics. All candidates had to reveal evidence that that they had resided continuously in the United States for five years. They also had to swear, and now and again display, that they were no longer anarchists or polygamists.

Finally, a super drop in African American electorate in the South occurred in the route of the first decade of the twentieth century. Every ex-Confederate u . S . A . Stripped blacks of their proper to vote through literacy exams, assets qualifications, and ballot taxes. During the 1870s, more than a hundred thirty,000 blacks had voted in Mississippi. That huge variety fell to as a minimum one,three hundred in 1900. During the Roosevelt years, whites used terror and lynching to intimidate black guys for the duration of the South. These movements decreased the sort of black electorate who might have licensed to test in beneath the modern prison tips. From 1900 to 1910, more than 1,3 hundred black guys were lynched and burned alive in southern and Midwestern states. Once blacks had been dropped from the vote casting rolls, registrars stripped many horrible and illiterate whites from the rolls inside the southern states, reducing the scale of the citizens even though similarly.

As result of those trends, voter participation prices fell from seventy nine percentage in 1896 to 65 percentage in 1904. The style never once more reached the excessive ranges appeared within the overdue nineteenth century.

Women's Suffrage

The most crucial exception to this fashion inside the direction of disenfranchisement changed into the growing suffrage movement for women. Although no states prolonged the vote to women eventually of the Roosevelt presidency, suffragette victories in Wyoming, Colorado, Idaho, and Utah within the course of the Eighteen Nineties picked up steam once more in the publish-Roosevelt years. Washington, California, Kansas, Oregon, and Arizona enfranchised women within the years from 1910 to 1912—growing a momentum that subsequently produced the Nineteenth Amendment (suffrage for women) in time for the election of 1920.

IMPACT AND LEGACY

Theodore Roosevelt is widely regarded due to the fact the number one contemporary President of america. The stature and have an effect on that the office has in recent times began out to expand with TR. Throughout the second half of of the 1800s, Congress have been the most powerful department of presidency. And despite the fact that the presidency started out out out to build up more energy in the course of the Eighteen Nineteen Eighties, Roosevelt completed the transition to a strong, effective executive. He made the President, in preference to the political events or Congress, the middle of American politics.

Roosevelt did this through the force of his person and through competitive authorities movement. He idea that the President had the right to apply any and all powers until they were in particular denied to him. He believed that as President, he had a very specific courting with and responsibility to the human beings, and therefore desired to task winning notions of restrained authorities and individualism; government, he maintained, should characteristic an agent of reform for the people.

His presidency endowed the innovative movement with credibility, lending the popularity of the White House to welfare law, government regulation, and the conservation movement. The choice to make society more sincere and equitable, with economic possibilities for all Americans, lay inside the returned of an awful lot of Roosevelt's program. The President moreover modified the authorities's dating to massive enterprise.

Prior to his presidency, the authorities had generally given the titans of company carte blanche to perform their dreams. Roosevelt believed that the authorities had the proper and the obligation to modify big corporation simply so its movements did not negatively have an impact on the general public. However, he in no way essentially challenged the reputation of big organization, believing that its existence marked a clearly happening section of the united states of a's economic evolution.

Roosevelt additionally revolutionized foreign affairs, believing that the us had a worldwide responsibility and that a sturdy foreign coverage served the united states of a's countrywide hobby. He have grow to be involved in Latin America with little hesitation: he oversaw the Panama Canal negotiations to endorse for U.S. Pastimes and intervened in Venezuela and Santo Domingo to hold balance inside the place. He furthermore worked with Congress to boost the U.S. Navy, which he believed need to deter potential enemies from centered on the us, and he carried out his energies to negotiating peace agreements, working to balance energy at some point of the area.

Even after he left place of work, Roosevelt persevered to paintings for his ideals. The Progressive Party's New Nationalism in 1912 released a power for protective federal law that seemed ahead to the innovative moves of the 1930s and the Nineteen Sixties. Indeed, Roosevelt's modern platform encompassed nearly every modern first-rate later enshrined within the New Deal of Franklin D. Roosevelt, the Fair Deal of Harry S. Truman, the New Frontier of John F. Kennedy, and the Great Society of Lyndon B. Johnson.

In phrases of presidential style, Roosevelt added "air of secrecy" into the political equation. He had a robust rapport with the general public and he understood a manner to use the media to shape public opinion.

He come to be the first President whose election changed into based totally absolutely extra at the individual than the political party. When human beings voted Republican in 1904, they had been usually casting their vote for Roosevelt the man or woman in area of for him because the equal antique-bearer of the Republican Party. The maximum famous President as much as his time, Roosevelt used his enthusiasm to win votes, to form problems, and to mold critiques in the way, he modified the government Place of work all of the time.

Chapter 6: Teddy As A Teenager

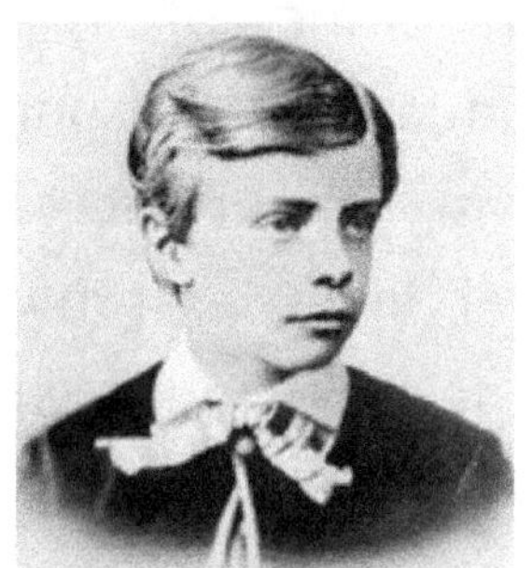

So some of the presidents of the 18th and nineteenth centuries were from hardscrabble beginnings, living a life of poverty as kids, however developing into self-made guys and ascending to the very superb place of business in the United States. Theodore Roosevelt come to be the exact opposite of that Lincolnian beginning as he changed into born into a rich own family in New York State on October 27, 1858. Teddy's father, Theodore Sr., become a famous and renowned businessman and philanthropist in New York City. His mother changed right into a southern belle from the Deep South who moved north just the remaining decade in advance than the outbreak of the Civil War to marry the rich Theodore Sr. Some of Teddy's earliest memories had been of his unreconstructed mother weaving memories of the vintage south and her lifestyles growing up on a plantation, a few element that the children loved, but the immoderate society of New York frowned upon.

Teddy's greater youthful lifestyles have become marked with the useful useful resource of ordinary struggling due to adolescence ailments, and masses of clinical docs and his parents alike feared that Teddy could not stay to inform the tale into adulthood. Teddy modified into frail from beginning and struggled to put on weight, generally being a slim toddler. To make topics worse, Teddy had horrible bronchial asthma, and in the nineteenth century, medical professionals have to do not some thing for him. According to Teddy in his later works, he may want to wake up within the middle of the night with the sensation of smothering to loss of existence, and the attacks had been so excessive that his parents notion he come to be about to die in the path of most of the episodes.

Given his scenario, Teddy became no longer like a number of the one-of-a-kind rich children in his portion of New York. He couldn't exit and hike and ride horses whenever he pleased due to his frail charter. This frailty drove Teddy to work and discover subjects that he became obsessed on, and from an early age he took a liking to the herbal pursuits. Young Teddy horrified his mother and the housekeepers even as he started out out to usher in quantities of lifeless animals to his room and started out schooling himself the art work of taxidermy. Roosevelt didn't care and endured to toil in his room for days on stop, cataloguing his findings and becoming greater inquisitive about the day. Though Teddy loved such hobbies, he still had a longing to be similar to the distinct boys, not stuck in his room for days on forestall, and he and his father worked diligently to help him be extra healthful.

Many wealthy human beings of the nineteenth century hired maids and nannies who raised their kids, and on the same time because the Roosevelts did rent assist, Teddy's mother and father have been active and loving people of their children's lives. The maximum hanging example of that love and devotion changed into the rich Theodore Sr. And his response to Teddy's allergic reactions. More regularly than no longer, the bronchial asthma attacks that Teddy suffered had been sooner or later of the late night time hours amongst nighttime and 6 a.M. Without fail, his father would possibly rush to his bedside and check at the unwell as he struggled to respire. Understanding that clean air need to assist a person coping with an allergies attack, Theodore Sr. Could tempo backward and forward sooner or later of their domestic with home windows open to herald smooth air. Theodore Sr. Spent hour after hour alongside along with his son, rubbing his chest and cuddling the kid until Teddy eventually determined his air and drifted off proper into a fitful sleep. For that devotion, Teddy back the love tenfold. His father supposed the whole thing to young Teddy, and Roosevelt wrote later that his father have emerge as the most type and mild soul that he had ever regarded. He additionally credited his father with being his position version for the relaxation of his existence. Teddy worked all of his days to make sure that he might be someone worth of being Theodore Roosevelt, Sr.'s son.

Through his father, Teddy began gaining knowledge of the route to manhood end up thru physical strength, power, and difficult work. During more than one journeys in the course of his younger life, Teddy tried to preserve tempo together alongside along with his in shape father on prolonged walks and hiking trips, and in time, the youngster began out to capture and subsequently surpass his father. After the ones bits of workout, Teddy located that his bronchial bronchial allergies slackened off, and he felt better both bodily and emotionally.

Teddy began out shaping every his highbrow and bodily being at a younger age, in his early young adults. He asked for and modified into given permission to hire a boxing teach while he misplaced a fight to a hard and speedy of boys. Teddy changed into so embarrassed via dropping the fight that he committed himself to becoming the first-class fighter that he must. Roosevelt have become happy that guys needed to be mentally and bodily in shape, and this was a perception that he saved with him at some stage in his whole existence.

Roosevelt also showed an important factor of his individual via his workout exercises and his time studying boxing: willpower. It might have been easy for a wealthy boy like Teddy to give up even as he failed, but he stored on pushing. It have end up this grit and resolution that laid the cornerstone for Teddy's adulthood, every inside the out of doors and political battles alike.

As Teddy grew into his past due teens, he have come to be a strapping more youthful man and one of the top notch athletes in his complete prolonged own family. It modified into additionally obvious that Teddy changed into brilliant in masses of educational aspects. He have end up an obsessive zoologist, even developing his non-public museum of taxidermy during his younger life. Teddy end up moreover a pace reader, and he used this capability to have a have a look at as many as books an afternoon. Through personal tutors, Roosevelt obtained the expertise had to start his research at Harvard University, and he entered the university within the 1870s.

While completing his first twelve months away at faculty, Teddy modified into dealt the worst blow of his lifestyles to that issue, as his father died . The truth that Teddy emerge as now not in a function to say a totally remaining farewell to his father haunted him for the rest of his days. The loss of his father might no longer be the best most important blow while it got here to Teddy's family life, as destiny might also need to have it. Roosevelt's person years have been marked thru method of personal loss, and his capability to conquer and persevere thru those tragedies. Roosevelt became a person of passion and emotional, however he worked diligently to suppress the emotions of anger and loss that he felt in the course of those darkish instances in his existence.

Striking Out on His Own

After burying his father, Teddy again to highschool and decided to give up his pursuit of the natural sciences, as an alternative that specialize in regulation. Teddy come to be a natural on this organisation, and he have emerge as a budding well-known person at Harvard, but the draw of home have come to be an excessive amount of, and in the long run Teddy transferred to Columbia to be towards his circle of relatives.

It changed into within the direction of this time at Columbia that Teddy started studying and writing his first ebook approximately the naval statistics of the War of 1812. Roosevelt have end up enthusiastic about the maritime records of america and the arena as a whole, and he became pretty of an professional inside the subject later in life. His e-book won huge reward after it have become posted, and hundreds of people credit score score his e-book with being the maximum authority on the naval battles of that conflict.

In his early 20s, Teddy have emerge as his attractions to politics, some thing that indignant the excessive society human beings in his internal circle, but he did not care. He grow to be obsessed on the idea of being a public determine. Teddy modified into constructed for the degree and public existence, and developing from a sick boy to a large, stout man, he towered over his contemporaries now not super bodily but collectively together with his persona. Roosevelt have become loud, gregarious, and outspoken, and whilst he talked, humans have been inquisitive about him. In brief, Roosevelt have become a born politician, and his adventure to the highest workplace within the land started in Albany, New York.

Roosevelt ran for, and was elected to the New York State Assembly in 1880, and he may additionally ultimately serve until 1884. From his first actual day in Albany, he rubbed many human beings the incorrect way. Teddy stimulated exceptional devotion from his admirers, however detractors hated him with a ardour. On his first day in Albany, Teddy walked into the chambers not like a meek guy on his first day at paintings, but as a person prepared to take the State Assembly through way of hurricane. Teddy wore his maximum expensive and flamboyant clothes, inflicting many within the chambers to assume he changed into no longer anything extra than a wealthy dandy from the town, however those detractors brief placed out that Roosevelt became now not handiest a person of pomp and situation however additionally a person of movement.

Chapter 7: Assemblyman Roosevelt

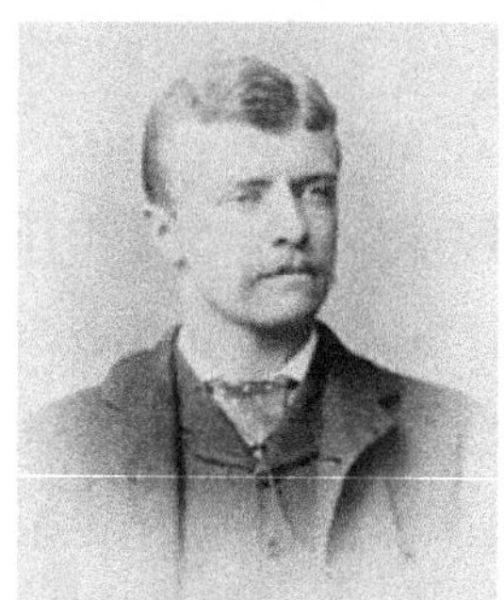

Immediately upon arriving in Albany, Teddy confirmed his propensity for attacking corruption. Roosevelt refused to hold the repute quo in regards to the corruption he noticed at some stage in the united states of america, and via the prevent of his very last time period, he had authored the most payments and tips of any assemblyman.

He have emerge as closest buddies with a consultant from the Adirondacks, and tended to desire representatives from New York's more rural districts. Roosevelt's largest enemies in workplace were people who represented the Irish Democratic political tool in New York's Tammany Hall. By the past due 19th century, political machines have been fueled through developing immigration charges, with the influx of Irish immigrants in New York City supporting propel the infamous Tammany Hall. A era later, Teddy's remote cousin Franklin can also need to interact in heated political battles with the Tammany device, now and again to his very very personal detriment.

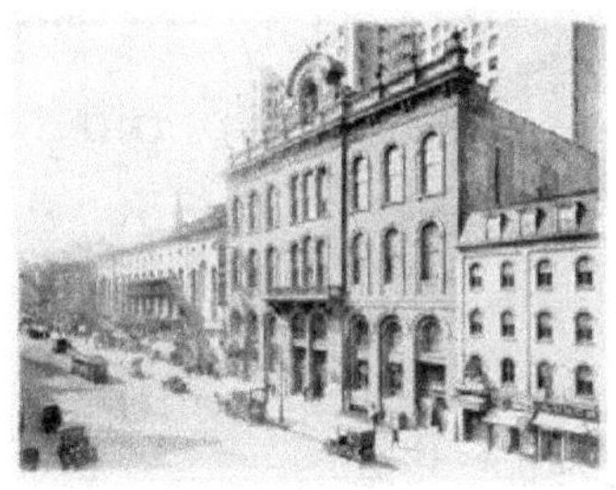

Tammany Hall in 1915

While Teddy changed into making his mark within the statewide political place, life took an surprising and terrible turn for the younger assemblyman. Teddy's extra youthful partner, Alice, changed into with infant in early 1884. The couple have grow to be excited to welcome their new addition into the sector, and in February it modified into time for her to offer starting. On February 12, 1884, Alice gave delivery to a healthful infant female who the couple named Alice after her mother. Directly after childbirth, the senior Alice have become ill and spent the following few days in an lousy lot ache in the Roosevelt home. On February 14, 1884, early in the morning, Teddy's mom died of typhoid fever inside the home. Grieving, Teddy walked the diverse bedsides of his daughter, his sick spouse, and his dying mother. Roosevelt loved his mother, and the dearth of her dealt him a savage blow.

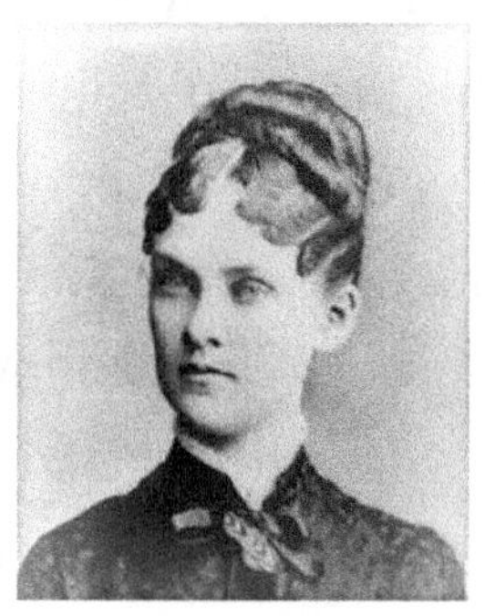

Alice

A dark day for Teddy emerge as only honestly starting, due to the reality at the same time as attending to the final requests of his mother in some unspecified time inside the future of the day, his spouse's fitness deteriorated due to the reality the day went on. In the overdue hours of February 14, Teddy's partner died at the same day as her mother in regulation. Theodore became beside himself, and the person who wrote huge magazine entries every day truly wrote a large X throughout his magazine that day, with the phrases, "The mild has long past from my life." Teddy struggled with the lack of his partner for the relaxation of his life, and will not even speak of her in later years. In the identical vein, he additionally had an emotional detachment from his daughter Alice. Many agree with that the pain of seeing his daughter have come to be too much to endure for him, and he didn't help decorate her till she became around the age of three or four. Men within the overdue nineteenth century had been not to reveal their feelings in a tremendous manner; it changed into visible as prone or fragile to cry and be damaged as he felt. Roosevelt did his first rate to cover his damage, however it simplest served to consume at him emotionally and purpose extra strain and pain in the course of this

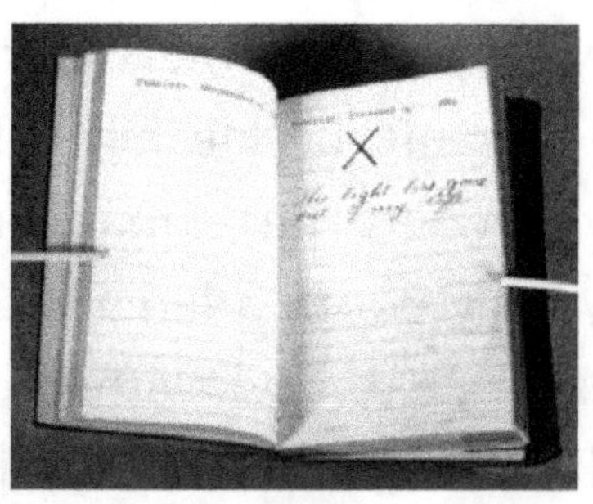

hard time.

After the deaths of his spouse and mom, Theodore did what he did great, paintings. Teddy became his interest to the approaching election season of 1884 and determined to take a vocal characteristic in ousting the incumbent Republican, Chester A. Arthur. Roosevelt determined Arthur as a do now not anything president and wanted to push for the election of George Edmonds from Vermont. Edmonds modified into a senator with a history of reform, and Roosevelt saw promise from his balloting record. Pushing hard at the New York Convention in opposition to Arthur, Roosevelt have come to be a pressure to be reckoned with on the nation diploma. The force of nature known as Theodore Roosevelt best persevered on the equal time as the Republican National Convention came about in Chicago later that 12 months. Fighting toward Arthur the complete time,

Roosevelt confirmed his political competencies thru swaying delegates to exchange their votes at some point of the method. Ultimately, Roosevelt's try have become for naught, and Arthur received the nomination during the convention.

After the conference, Roosevelt confronted a difficult preference. He did no longer like James Blaine or Chester Arthur, the Republican charge tag, but many inside the Republican Party wanted Roosevelt to aid the rate price tag publically. Roosevelt understood that birthday celebration politics known as for him to help the eventual candidate, but Roosevelt emerge as not a person of traditional notion. Ultimately even though, Roosevelt subsidized the Republican rate price ticket and moved onto extra adventures.

Heading West

Roosevelt might later write, "Only if you've been to the bottom valley can you apprehend how amazing it's far to be on the highest mountain pinnacle", a quote that would later infamously make its way into Richard Nixon's resignation speech. But on the time, understandably, Roosevelt felt a chunk of his existence had dimmed. He decided to transport away New York and politics inside the returned of; besides, he had constantly believed politics have become a career incorrect to maintaining a livelihood. With his love for the united states over the city on the principle edge of his mind, Roosevelt determined to head away the large metropolis, and the West modified into the proper location to do it.

Roosevelt become a rich aristocrat from New York City and to say that he caught out like a sore thumb inside the rugged Dakota Territory is a massive understatement, however he did no longer care. He dressed the detail, appeared the part, and straight away began out out large sport hunts in the course of the Territory. While in the

Dakotas, Roosevelt have grow to be a remarkable discern in the politics of the Territory, helping the ranchers shape organizations. Roosevelt moreover cherished taking place huge sport hunts and being far from the life that he become aware about. Roosevelt thrived in the West, surrounded with the useful resource of grand vistas and large open regions. He spent days at a time on horseback, monitoring big recreation and starting efforts to keep big game and lands from increase.

Life in the Wild West grow to be no a great deal less wild for Roosevelt than for all of us else. He served as Deputy Sheriff of the northern a part of his u.S. Of the united states beneath Sheriff "Hell Roaring" Bill Jones. His relationship with the Sheriff and all different participants of his tiny frontier society were very well democratic. This became, of direction, in stark evaluation to the carefully classist Victorian society of

New York City. Although Roosevelt come to be the Sheriff's inferior in regulation enforcement, Jones though worked as a farm animals hand on Roosevelt's ranch.

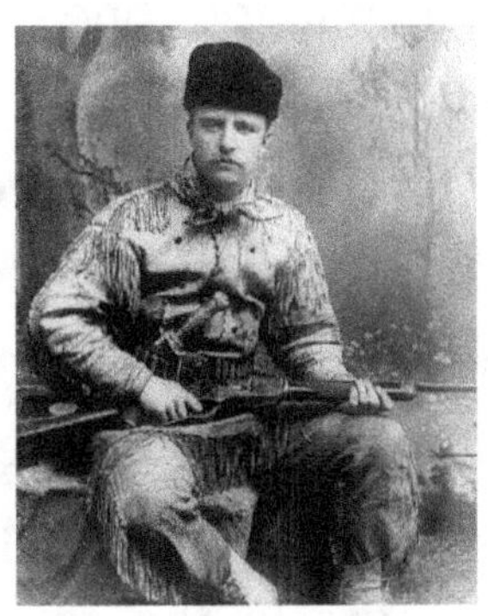

Teddy in 1885

Roosevelt additionally took the day out west to turn out to be a sincere extra avid reader and creator. He take a look at through the use of the usage of the campfire on the same time as out on the direction and sat on his the the the front porch for hours on quit, analyzing into the wee hours of the night time. Roosevelt decided to begin logging his adventures of the West and sat proper right down to write approximately his reviews. Ultimately, he produced three books approximately the frontier.

Roosevelt's time within the Dakotas proved to be a very formidable one in his political development. Having grown up among wealth and privilege, Roosevelt can also want to have effortlessly continued to isolate and alienate himself from mainstream American society. Moving West, however, gave him the opportunity to go away his roots in the returned of and befriend a class of Americans he in any other case may need to by no means have seemed.

Chapter 8: New Political Ambitions

Refreshed, and with a new outlook on lifestyles, Roosevelt left the Dakotas and reduce lower back to his existence in New York. Teddy had decided that there had been political arenas which have been unchallenged, and he became lonely. It have become time to surround himself alongside collectively together with his circle of relatives, and supply marriage each other try. Also, Teddy's wreck from the political arena left him longing for the antique feeling, and he changed into organized to take the following step in his public existence.

Upon returning to New York, Teddy rekindled an vintage early life romance with Edith Carow. Roosevelt asked her to marry him, and barely years after losing his first wife, Roosevelt wed Edith. Ironically, Edith have been a traveller at Teddy's and Alice's bridal ceremony reception years earlier. Upon his cross again to New York, the two brief started out courting and went to London in late 1886 after the mayoral election. The couple have been given married remote places and toured Europe for 15 weeks on their honeymoon. They would possibly ultimately have 5 kids.

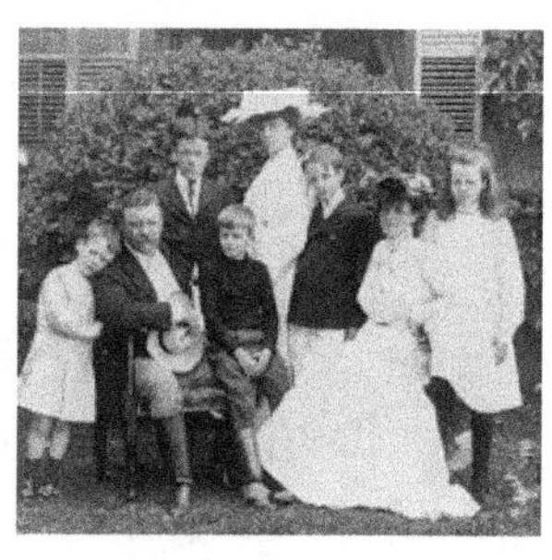

The Roosevelt family in 1903: (from L-R) Quentin, Teddy, Ted Jr., "Archie", Alice, Kermit, Edith, and Ethel

Roosevelt ran for Mayor of New York City in 1886 and got here in zero.33 out of three primary candidates. This humiliated him, but he persevered to fight on. Teddy got his huge political harm with the following presidential election; Benjamin Harrison ran towards James Blaine for the Republican rate tag. Once once more, Roosevelt went within the course of the kingdom in manual for Blaine's opponent. The long-shot Harrison not simplest defeated Blaine for the Republican nomination but gained the White House.

Roosevelt's artwork inside the Republican number one did no longer pass ignored with the useful resource of using the trendy president, and Roosevelt have become asked to Washington D.C. To sign up for the Civil Service Commission. The assignment became quality for the reform-minded Roosevelt, and he started out without delay to make his mark in Washington. Roosevelt grow to be now not some thing if now not audacious; he started out his new activity seeking to weed out patronage jobs inside the route of the country. One wonders if he belief for a moment that his technique became a patronage decide on, however each manner, Roosevelt wasn't through that fact, and he constantly butted heads with the very nice-rating officials. Through it all, he remained a reformer, and people decent that in the late nineteenth century. Roosevelt stored his function subsequently of the Harrison presidency or maybe spent a few years of Grover Cleveland's presidency within the same feature.

Eventually, Roosevelt fed up in the pastime and longed to move decrease back home to New York. Once again in New York, Roosevelt landed an possibility afforded to him thru using his hard paintings in the Civil Service Commission. In 1894, the Republicans won control of New York City, and the mayor-pick out ran on a reform platform. Roosevelt in shape the bill flawlessly for a place in his authorities. Though Roosevelt had no enjoy with regulation enforcement ahead, the mayor appointed him to the police rate. Roosevelt have come to be speedy elected to the control of the police rate, so he became something of a police leader of the metropolis. The New York Police Department come to be idea via manner of many to be the maximum useless, corrupt and worthless police branch within the complete United States. Roosevelt made it his assignment to reform the police at each level, from the way in which patrolmen have been selected and knowledgeable to the very nice degrees of the branch's propensity for patronage and returned-slapping promotions.

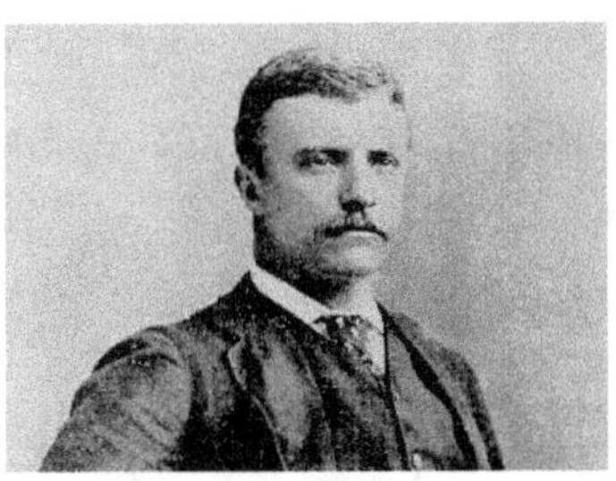

Commissioner Roosevelt

Roosevelt moreover heard thru many informants that police officers on the midnight shift may want to discover a pleasant alley, prop up a stool and sleep the night time away. Not only were his officials lazy, however they had been additionally on the take as nicely. Corruption ran rampant, so Roosevelt decided he needed to rule with an iron fist, and positioned into effect one of the maximum hated legal guidelines at the books of New York City, the dry Sunday law. Saloons overlooked the dry Sunday ordinance, and virtually paid off police officers to live open and serve the thirsty after church. Roosevelt started a marketing campaign to bust all the unlawful saloons open on Sunday. This served a dual purpose: it took illegal bribes out of his officers' pockets and made the newspapers. Roosevelt come to be an uncanny baby-kisser and understood that the click constantly favored to drum up public useful resource for any reforms he proposed.

Roosevelt started a massive media advertising campaign to smooth up the New

York Police Department, not via hiding the troubles inner his branch, but thru using displaying the disasters in stark reality. Roosevelt commenced taking journalists on nighttime strolls via the worst neighborhoods of the town, and countless instances they positioned officials asleep or off obligation in bars or different establishments. Roosevelt labored tirelessly to clean up the police department and received a whole lot brilliant press and political momentum from his time as Police Commissioner. While Roosevelt have become a a hit commissioner, he had his eyes set inside the route of a cross lower back to Washington, and backstage he have become the use of his Republican friends to gain a seat within the subsequent Republican government on a rustic large degree.

By the quit of his tenure with the New York Police Department, Roosevelt became brief becoming a family name. What have become as soon as the maximum corrupt and useless regulation enforcement organisation within the kingdom had transitioned into an example of a police strain that labored for the not unusual well. The town's police were held to higher necessities; Roosevelt made wonderful they had been really patrolling when they have been presupposed to be, a common problem before his tenure. And police hostels which had housed policeman while they were supposedly "on duty" have been closed. Roosevelt's strictness and hard regulations ensured that the dominion's fastest growing town become now not ridden with crime and lack of self notion.

A National Politican

Election season dawned all over again in 1896, and Roosevelt once more decided to be a prime player within the political area. The Republican candidate grow to be William McKinley, and whilst the Democratic candidate changed into the socialist William Jennings Bryan, Roosevelt believed that Bryan modified into unstable to the united states and end up on the lookout for to wreck the American manner of existence. Bryan had many supporters within the West and Midwest because of the reality he used his recommendations to gain farmer and decrease center-class voters on his facet.

Roosevelt took to the national campaign direction, giving dozens of stump speeches for William McKinley. During the Eighteen Nineties, it modified into taken into consideration unseemly for the presidential applicants to go out on the talking route for themselves, in order that they relied on their political allies to exit and drum up help for his or her cause. Roosevelt worked tirelessly to drum up manual for McKinley, and ultimately McKinley received the election in a landslide in competition to Bryan. McKinley preferred the guide of Roosevelt, however he changed into moreover cautious of the reformer because he have become seen as an in depth of the Republican Party. Roosevelt's buddies, consisting of Henry Cabot Lodge, began to press McKinley for a method inside the authorities for Roosevelt. He had earned the possibility to work in Washington manner to his hard paintings, his buddies argued, and McKinley in the long run relented and gave Roosevelt a hobby as Assistant Secretary of the Navy.

If McKinley modified into concerned approximately young Roosevelt jogging amok in Washington, he gave him the perfectly wrong interest. Roosevelt became the Assistant Secretary of the Navy, however the Secretary of the Navy become ill and did now not even come into the offices for days at a time, giving Roosevelt entire manage over the Naval Department. Roosevelt headed a pinnacle naval buildup of battleships at a few stage within the primary months of his tenure and started out to set his points of interest foreign places. Roosevelt changed into an expansionist; similarly to enforcing the Monroe Doctrine, Roosevelt believed American forces need to set up colonies as Great Britain did. The Assistant Secretary of the Navy started sending messages to the White House approximately the dangers of the ever-growing unrest in Cuba. Roosevelt believed that the united states need to assist the Cubans benefit independence from Spain.

McKinley favored no a part of the developing battle lots less than 100 miles from his u . S . A ., however in 1898 he now not had a choice after an American deliver in Havana Harbor named the united statesMaine exploded, killing rankings of sailors. The Spanish had been right now blamed, and the warfare hawks of the usa had their justification for war.

Teddy Roosevelt refused to overlook out on his possibility for glory. One of the elements of Theodore Sr.'s life that caught with him and his son became the fact that the senior Roosevelt did not serve inside the American Civil War. Roosevelt Sr. Turned into of age, but he had used his wealth to buy a alternative in the ranks. Roosevelt did go to infinite battlefields along with his philanthropic artwork and helped many human beings in need in a few unspecified time within the future of the war, however it became a black mark on his life that he in no manner forgave himself for. Teddy would possibly no longer make the identical mistake that his father made. Immediately after the warfare became declared by way of of Congress, Teddy resigned his cushty venture in the Naval Department and volunteered his offerings to the usa as a soldier.

Though he had zero experience in war, he used his stature to advantage the colonelcy of what need to end up referred to as the Rough Riders. Teddy recruited his private particular combination of infantrymen ranging from New York aristocrats who rode the finest horseflesh and had Tiffany chinaware of their commissary wagons, to tough men from the Dakotas who've been appropriate with a gun. Roosevelt paid for a number of the costs out of his very very own pocket and right now moved to the southern coast of Florida to locate transportation to the island nation.

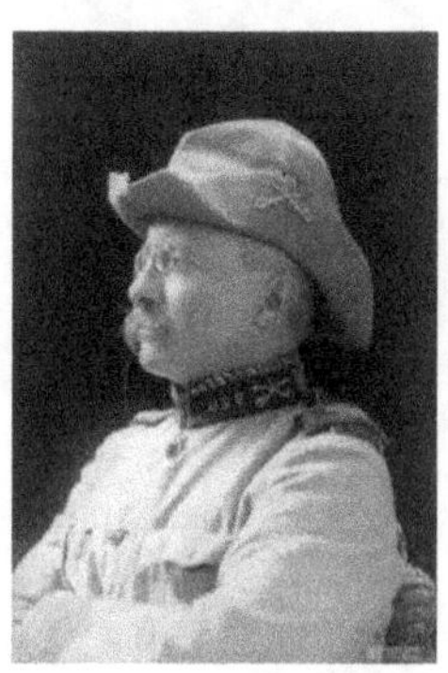

Teddy should regularly be known as Colonel in the years after his presidency.

Though many credit rating rating the Rough Riders for a fee up San Juan Heights, it changed into their charge up Kettle Hill in the course of a warfare that won the regiment popularity and renown at some degree within the Army. Teddy led from the the front, passing into the road of fireside a unstable amount of instances as he led from the the front. The Rough Riders carried the hill and carried the day on the battlefield.

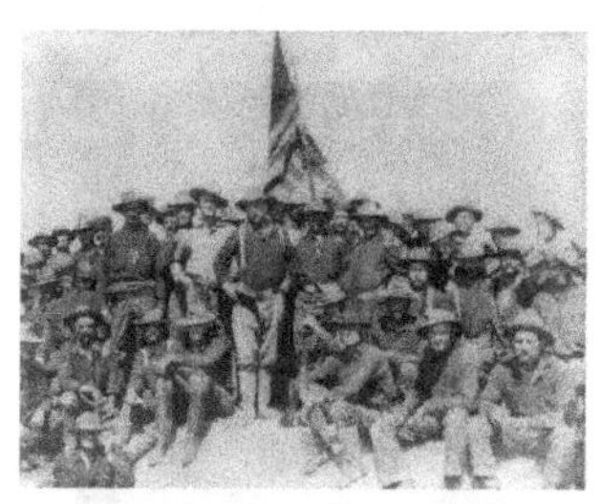

Chapter 9: The Rough Riders On San Juan Hill

The conflict changed into short and comparatively cold for the Americans, and the victory inside the Spanish-American War set the usa at the expansionist route Roosevelt preferred.

Upon his bypass again to america, Roosevelt have become lauded as a hero, and the New York Republican tool sought to coins in on his fame. The Republicans nominated Roosevelt for Governor in 1898, and he won the election, taking his place on the top of the New York authorities in Albany. In his time because of the reality the governor, Roosevelt fought business enterprise trusts and corruption in country authorities, and he made buddies with diverse people of the clicking. Roosevelt held press conferences a day, which have become savvy. Constantly giving the click duplicate, he ensured favorable critiques, and he might also additionally want to persuade the click to print the styles of tales he had to painting.

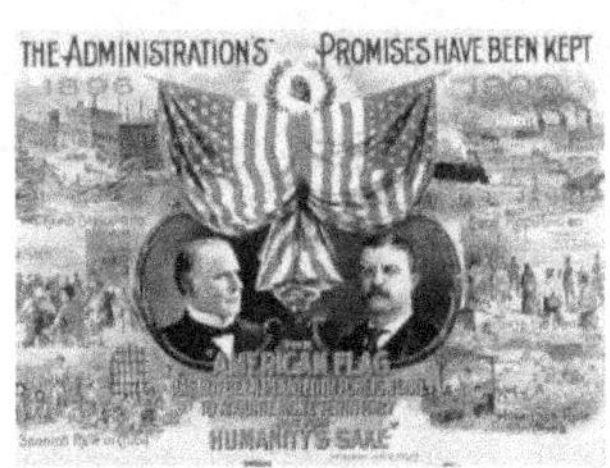

Roosevelt's New York enemies was hoping to rid the dominion in their progressive governor, but that might be tons much less difficult stated than done. Governor Roosevelt grow to be very famous and might genuinely be difficult to triumph over as an incumbent in 1902. Machine and business organisation pastimes devised an thrilling answer in the summer time of 1900. At the Republican National Convention in Philadelphia, the New York gadget leaders determined to sell Roosevelt for the Vice Presidency. Doing so should do away with him from New York. Furthermore, the Vice President became notoriously insignificant in national politics. Machinists for this reason notion that making Roosevelt the Vice President might flip him into a no one.

The machinists, led via Senator Thomas Platt of New York, encountered a trouble: McKinley's advertising campaign chief, Mark Hanna, did not suppose Roosevelt might also need to make a high-quality addition to the Republican charge tag. The machinists, but, managed to steer Hanna and most different delegations at the National Convention that Roosevelt changed into the ideal addition to the GOP rate tag. Roosevelt turned into first of all uncertain of the placement. While many perception it'd surrender his political profession, Roosevelt wasn't even positive which have turn out to be a awful issue. Perhaps it have become time to move lower back to the nation-state, except.

After a few convincing, Roosevelt because of this acquainted the nomination as Vice President alongside President McKinley. The pair obtained the election of 1900, making Roosevelt the Vice President in March of 1901.

It speedy became apparent even though, that Teddy changed into meant for even higher workplace, and as 1900 rolled spherical, his name began to be thrown spherical on the countrywide degree.

In the months after his reelection and 2nd inauguration, President McKinely deliberate a excursion for the duration of the us, with the very last forestall coming on the Pan-American Exposition in Buffalo, New York. Expos had been well-known techniques for towns to provide themselves on national and global ranges, making them perfect activities for presidents to wait. McKinley additionally cherished greeting the general public, which concerned his safety team of workers. By the time he gave a speech at the Expo on September five, 1901, his protection had been doubled.

The following day, McKinley took a journey to Niagara Falls in advance than returning to the Expo. While on his way to the Temple of Music, anarchist Leon Czolgosz were given inner issue easy sort of the president and shot him twice inside the chest. McKinley changed into aware enough to implore the institution not to rip Czolgosz limb to limb, and within the days after the taking pictures he regarded to be at the direction to healing. In reality, Vice President Roosevelt went on a tenting trick to the Adirondack Mountains in upstate New York on the same time as McKinley endured his convalescence.

As it have become out, clinical docs did now not have the vital generation to locate the bullet despite the fact that lodged in McKinley's abdomen, and the sunny prognostications that they stored making to reassure the overall public have been faux choice. Ironically, a new invention, a primitive shape of an X-ray device, changed into on the Expo grounds, but it couldn't be relied on for use. Doctors had no concept that McKinley emerge as appreciably ill till gangrene made him take a flip for the more serious approximately per week after he became shot. On September 14, 1901, President McKinley died.

In one of the best ironies of electoral records, President McKinley became shot six months after Roosevelt's assumption of the Vice Presidency, catapulting Theodore Roosevelt into the White House. This turned into a much cry from what the machinists had intended: in place of consigning him into a political abyss, Roosevelt modified into now the handiest man or woman inside the United States.

President Roosevelt

The vice presidency was the worst undertaking for Teddy Roosevelt. Essentially a figurehead role, he bored rapid along together with his pastime of presiding over the Senate. Teddy changed into bored in Washington and involved he changed into in a terrible political spot. In 1901, Teddy figured the most effective saving grace modified into that he may use the location to vault himself into the White House in 1904.

After succeeding the slain McKinley, Roosevelt hit the floor taking walks for the duration of his presidency, and have become one of the maximum lively presidents each earlier than or after his phrases. He took his love for agree with-busting and his love for reform to the country wide degree. Roosevelt tackled the maximum implementing of corporations very early on in his presidency: Standard Oil. Led by way of John D. Rockefeller, Standard Oil had a virtual monopoly on all the important oil refineries and oil drilling portions of the united states. Roosevelt noticed Standard Oil for what it modified into - an illegal agree with - and have grow to be determined to interrupt up the industrial corporation corporation's massive holdings. He succeeded in which awesome reform-minded presidents had failed.

Big business enterprise did no longer care a great deal for the reform-minded president, but he had the political pull and intelligence to skip all of their tries to preserve the reputation quo. He have become the number one president to take an lively detail in tough work negotiations even as a coal miner strike threatened to depart masses of thousands at a few level within the u.S. Without coal to warm temperature their homes. While many have been greatly surprised that Teddy sided with the industrial enterprise hobbies in that particular case, he noticed it as his obligation as president to make certain that the human beings of the us had coal for heat in the upcoming wintry weather.

Roosevelt endured his love for the outside and the West, and he took primary steps to make certain that the beauty of those lands may be round for future generations to revel in. He became the primary president to signal law shielding monuments in the route of the u . S . A . And helped set up the National Park Service that still protects the splendor and surroundings of the USA to these days.

Another difficulty of every day life that Roosevelt sought to restore end up the concept of safe foods and drinks for the country. The United States did now not have a Food and Drug Administration all through the early 20th century, which means there have been no officials ensuring that the businesses that produced meals have been doing so in a secure way. After the debatable, eye-putting in place ebook by means of using Upton Sinclair, The Jungle, uncovered the horrors of the Chicago meatpacking employer, the meals industry got here below fireplace. Always the opportunist, Roosevelt observed the campaign for stable meals as every different way to gain amazing press and get famous help on his issue. Roosevelt spearheaded the Pure Food and Drug Act, which ensured that corporations stored a smooth operation and that they classified their products efficiently. For goodbye at a few degree in the early records of the u . S ., quack remedies need to declare some component on their bottles that had been sold in a few unspecified time inside the destiny of the United States. A "marvel elixir" may be not anything but natural alcohol, due to the fact the labels had been no longer standardized. Many human beings have been taking in huge quantities of medication which encompass morphine and cocaine in the ones popular, patent tablets, and Roosevelt's Act destroyed the opportunities of those agencies getting away with such backhanded practices.

Roosevelt also finished his dream of seeing the USA emerge as a global player. In 1905, the Russians and the Japanese went to war over disputed territories, and the struggle dragged on with out an result in sight. Roosevelt thought that with the useful resource of using implementing American will at the struggle, he could not handiest increase the united states of the usa's reach but moreover set the u . S . A . Up for further diplomatic treaties that would gain the USA. Calling the Russians and the Japanese to the bargaining table, Roosevelt met them in New Hampshire and refused to permit them to go away till an settlement become made. The facets diagnosed Roosevelt as their mediator, and via his diligence, the Russo- Japanese War came to an stop. For his art work in turning in peace to the Far East, Roosevelt have become the first sitting president to be provided the Nobel Peace Prize.

In go back, the us changed into granted permission to construct, run, and percentage in the earnings of a canal that would join the Atlantic and Pacific Oceans. Roosevelt observed the opportunity to make the us the fantastic naval strength in the global, by means of using linking his coasts with a shorter path. Before the canal have become built, ships had to bypass all the way to the lowest of South America to sail to California. Now that the canal became constructed, it took months off sailing instances, and it brought america tens of millions of bucks in brought income.

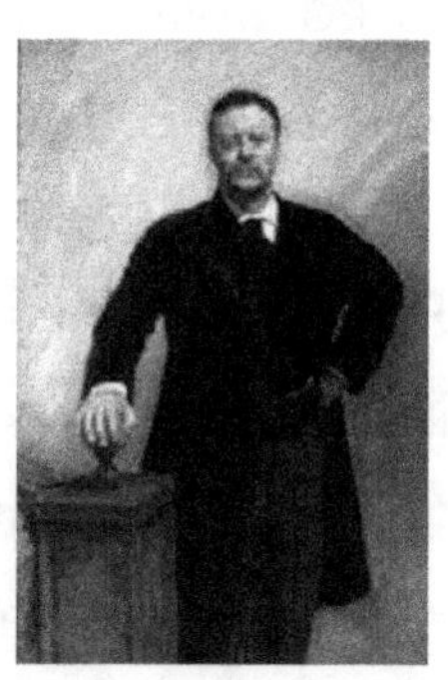

Chapter 10: 1903 Presidential Portrait Of Roosevelt

Roosevelt visiting the Panama Canal below production in 1906

Although Roosevelt had most effective been elected president as quickly as, he had served almost 8 years and followed precedent with the beneficial aid of no longer taking walks for reelection in 1908. Instead, Teddy left the White House for William Howard Taft. President Taft had received Roosevelt's private guide in 1908, and the preceding president modified into happy to vacate the White House to make room for Taft. This political alliance, but, may destroy in a massive way in 1912.

Final Years

For the time, though, Roosevelt centered on his vintage flame: nature and looking. Instead of in fact searching inside the Adirondacks, as he frequently had, Roosevelt determined to embark on a trip to Africa. In 1909, right now after leaving the White House, Roosevelt headed for contemporary-day-day Kenya. His searching day trip, but, should take him thru a exquisite bulk of Africa, as he ventured into the crucial Congo and up via cutting-edge Sudan. Always the preservationist, Roosevelt amassed specimens to deliver again to america for safety in the Smithsonian Natural History Museum. In the forestall, this covered almost 12,000

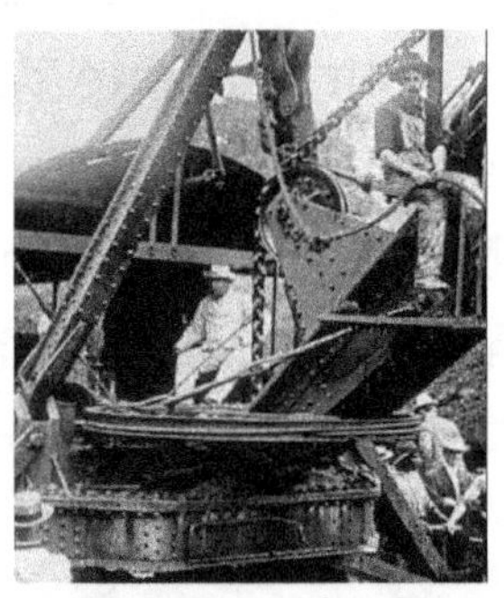

animals and insects, which includes over 500 big sport mammals. Hunting elephants, rhinos and hippos thrilled Roosevelt greater than any of the political squabbles he encountered in politics.

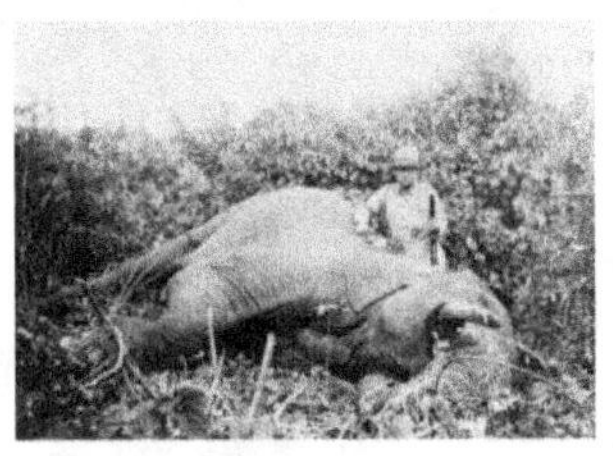

Roosevelt searching elephants on safari

As President, Roosevelt had emerge as a life-prolonged member of the National Rifle Association. Hunting became genuinely his ardour, and he authored many books at the topics in advance than and after his Presidency, which encompass Through the Brazilian Wilderness, an account of his zoological trek via Brazil

In 1908, Roosevelt toyed with the idea of strolling for a third time period. He knew he may also additionally want to without trouble win reelection, but he had pledged not to are in search of for greater time as President on the same time as he ran in 1904. He consequently opted out and handpicked Howard Taft as his successor, believing him to be a dedicated cutting-edge.

After his safari adventure, but, Roosevelt toured Europe, wherein he found greater approximately happenings in American politics because of the fact his departure. Many progressives contacted him expressing their issues about the Taft Presidency. Roosevelt consequently opted to move again to the usa to figure things out for himself.

By past due 1910, Roosevelt revised his opinion on Taft. He wrote Senator Henry Cabot Lodge, announcing "I in the end needed to admit that he [Taft] had lengthy beyond wrong on sure elements; and I then moreover needed to admit to myself that deep down below I had all alongside diagnosed he come to be wrong." Thus, Roosevelt determined to u.S.A. Taft and are searching out the Presidency himself. Understanding the gravity of his choice,

Roosevelt titled this financial break of his autobiography "Armageddon and Afterward."

Roosevelt to start with hesitated, but. He opted into the Republican nominating approach past due in 1911. Regardless, Roosevelt become capable of win nine of the thirteen Presidential Primaries, and it changed into one of the first elections to apply the way to lease a candidate. The final states, however, persisted to allow Republican politicians to decide the destiny of their delegates. As such, Taft now managed the celebration's energy marketers and grow to be able to narrowly ordinary the nomination over Roosevelt on the country wide convention. Befriending politicians had in no manner been Roosevelt's robust match.

Roosevelt for this reason encountered a trouble, one that had typically plagued his political existence: he changed into widely well-known with the general public but have become disdained through his fellow politicians, a predicament that had delivered him to the Vice Presidency within the first area. But the previous president did not surrender then. Roosevelt took his supporters out of the Republican National Convention in protest and fashioned his personal Progressive Party. When Teddy proclaimed he grow to be "as in form as a bull moose," the party have come to be called the "Bull Moose Party."

Roosevelt's proposals throughout the nomination combat and the overall election have been a number of his maximum radical. He railed toward the "unholy" alliance of government and organisation interests and accused them of maintaining a "sinister affect or control of specific pursuits" over countrywide government. As president he became genuinely a populist, however as a presidential candidate in 1912 he transformed into the populist's populist.

The former president become now labelled an extensive. To this he wrote, "The grievance had been made from me that I am a radical. So I am. I couldn't be some thing else, feeling as I do. But I am a radical who most earnestly desires to see the novel programme accomplished via conservatives." In his attacks, Roosevelt did now not maintain again. He brazenly railed in opposition to particular agencies and conglomerates, which includes Standard Oil and U.S. Steel.

On October 14th, 1912, however, Roosevelt's marketing advertising and marketing marketing campaign have come to be added to an sad stop, albeit one which solidified the Roosevelt legend. Roosevelt have become in Milwaukee to supply a advertising advertising marketing campaign speech while a nearby barkeep named John Schrank caught wind of Roosevelt's vicinity and shot him as he changed into leaving a motel to supply the speech on the

Milwaukee Auditorium. Thankfully, the bullet passed through a folded up replica of Roosevelt's 50 page speech and his eyeglass case in advance than inns in his ribcage quick of his lungs or coronary coronary coronary heart. An adept hunter and a few element of a scientist, Roosevelt observed he became now not coughing blood and concluded that the bullet should now not have penetrated a crucial organ. In his everyday cowboy-like style, Roosevelt refused to visit the hospital and introduced the speech with blood seeping via his blouse. He brought to the target market that he have been shot, pronouncing "it takes a couple of bullet to kill a Bull Moose."

John Schrank

Roosevelt went to the health facility quickly after the assassination try and remained there for nearly each week. Taft and challenger Woodrow Wilson halted their campaigns in honor of the previous president, high-quality resuming them even as Roosevelt resumed his.

The assassination strive, however, did now not rally the American people round Roosevelt. On Election Day, he came in 2d in the back of Wilson, with 27% of the vote, the most a 3rd party candidate had ever gained. Incumbent President Taft came in 0.33, making him the primary president looking for reelection to lose with the aid of the use of coming in 0.33 in choice to second. However, the cut up within the Republican Party had surpassed the presidency to a Democrat. President Wilson became the primary -term Democratic President due to the reality earlier than the Civil War.

The defeat proved to be Roosevelt's very last foray in politics, however Roosevelt continued to rail toward Wilson at a few level in the the relaxation of his existence. He antagonistic the President's timidity on warfare in Europe and endorsed rapid US intervention there. When the U.S. In the stop did enter the struggle, Roosevelt furnished to create a volunteer regiment and serve on the the front, however Wilson rejected his request, rightly believing the preceding president to be too vintage and susceptible. Several of Teddy's sons did fight in World War I, and his youngest son Quentin emerge as killed in 1918 even as flying a undertaking over France.

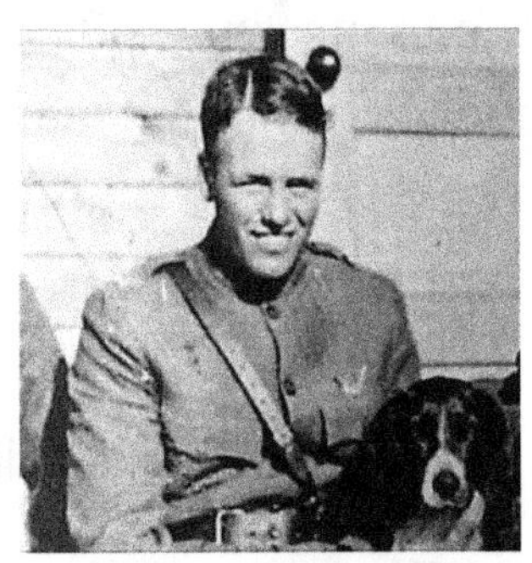

Lieutenant Quentin Roosevelt in France, 1917

Wilson's evaluation of Roosevelt's fitness proved accurate. On January 6, 1919, Teddy Roosevelt died of a coronary coronary

coronary heart attack on the age of 60. He had remained lively till the prevent of his existence, and lots of speculated he might also need to are searching out the presidency yet again inside the election of 1920. For the kingdom, Roosevelt's death changed into surprising. He became buried close to his cherished domestic in Oyster Bay, Sagamore Hill. As a quit end result of his loss of life, the Roosevelt circle of relatives received severa telegrams expressing their unhappiness on the dearth of the president. Although he had out of place the election in 1912, Roosevelt changed into without a doubt the us of a's maximum famous politician while he died, and few presidents had been capable of in shape his popularity due to the reality. He have become speedy honored throughout the dominion, most famously thru the usage of being carved into Mount Rushmore less than twenty years after his death.

The legacy of Theodore Roosevelt is type of now not viable to absolutely degree. He finished lots in his lifestyles that it took 3 complete books for famend biographer Edmund Morris to inform his tale. Roosevelt turn out to be a person of movement and someone of passion; from his earliest years, he knew that the manner to make a place for himself within the international end up thru way of doing. From his earliest years as an asthmatic boy who taught himself a way to be physical healthy, to his climb up the political ladder, Roosevelt normally did it his manner.

Chapter 11: His Birth And Early Life

Theodore Roosevelt changed into born in New York City on October, 27th 1858. He have become born at 28 East twentieth Street and have become the second one of 4 children born to Theodore and Martha Bulloch Roosevelt. His circle of relatives have been associated with the Dutch that had moved into the vicinity in the seventeenth century. According to loads of resources, his start come to be easy for his mom.[1] At this factor, it would were clean to count on that this infant might be not anything too unique and will skip without delay to absorb an energetic feature in the own family and their way of life.

Considering the period we are talking about, Roosevelt changed into born proper proper into a mainly wealthy family, way to his father being a a hit businessman that imported glass further to a burgeoning philanthropist. Indeed, his father have become one of the maximum well-known philanthropists in that a part of the us of the united states. His mother, alternatively, have turn out to be at the begin from Georgia, in which she had grown up on a plantation. It is stated that she regularly struggled with having moved up to now north, but correctly stuck it out for the sake of her marriage and circle of relatives.

By all bills, the daddy of Roosevelt have turn out to be a robust person and it has formerly been stated that he modified into the exceptional individual that Roosevelt in truth feared in his existence. His father become taken into consideration as being an energetic character in addition to a dominant determine, so it is simple to look how he must have played a number one feature inside the life of Roosevelt. However, whilst he stated that he became afraid of his father, we are not certain as to what precisely he meant with the aid of the usage of that word. His father turn out to be a domineering person, although we are able to see, at the equal time as we paintings through his story, this have become a personality that might expand inside the extra youthful Roosevelt as properly, even though it may be utilized in a miles greater inexperienced manner.

Roosevelt had an older sister known as Anna. He changed into then accompanied by means of manner of a greater youthful brother by way of manner of the selection of Elliot and in the long run a extra youthful sister called Corinne. However, we apprehend little about his interplay along along with his siblings, as maximum of the reminiscences about the young Roosevelt are, of course, focused via and large on him as an individual. There are not any indicators that he had anything aside from a warmth dating with them.

From an early age, Roosevelt have turn out to be affectionately regarded with the aid of the use of the nickname of 'Teedie'; not a million miles a ways from the decision he might also become regarded with the useful resource of later on in life. Even despite the fact that he turn out to be born into what many observed as being the right own family, the more youthful Roosevelt frequently suffered from infection that, at times, end up near to being deadly. In precise, Roosevelt had problems with allergic reactions, and this affected the way in which he became able to have interaction with others. It changed into additionally the cause why Roosevelt have turn out to be truly informed at domestic, in region of blending with one of a kind kids, as it become felt that it become too unstable for his health to be surrounded with the aid of too many particular humans.

As a little one, it is regarded that he loved taking element in highbrow sports, probable because it changed into as an opportunity hard for him to have a love of more strenuous sports activities, because of his hypersensitive reactions. He is known to have had a love of books and could spend a massive amount of time every reading nature via literature further to moving into the super out of doors as a way to absorb what became round him. This have turn out to be some thing that might bypass without delay to have an impact in his lifestyles in a while, however this is one area that we're able to find out in greater detail in addition on inside the ebook.

Issues with the Civil War

The 1860's have been a tough time inside the U.S. Thanks to the Civil War and it become specially hard for the Roosevelt circle of relatives. His father changed into seasoned-Union and worked at the side of President Lincoln because of a preference to enhance the lives of each Union squaddies and their families. On the possibility hand, his mom, maternal grandmother, and aunt were all sending programs lower back to own family that have been in the back of enemy traces, as they had been all Southern women.

This introduced about some tension inside the family, but for Roosevelt, it come to be additionally a as an opportunity exciting time. It is thought that he cherished the secrecy of effectively smuggling these manual applications inside the decrease back of enemy lines. But on the identical time, he held sturdy thoughts of turning into a Union soldier and a battle hero. It end up a time of combined messages, despite the fact that the more youthful Roosevelt need to no longer grow to be an person who might be defined as sending out blended messages to people that he might go without delay to serve.

However, truely the younger Roosevelt became despite the fact that of an age in which he became not able to clearly realise what grow to be taking region within the u.S., or the issues inside his circle of relatives, leaving him specially oblivious to the diverse problems due to the Civil War. Overall, this a part of his lifestyles may want to no longer bypass without delay to shape his mind regarding battle, this is as an alternative sudden, considering that he would possibly emerge as quick to throw out the idea of america using its navy talents when he worked his way proper into a function of strength.

Moving into the Teenage Years.

As the more youthful Roosevelt moved into his teenage years what we see is a younger guy that took the advice of his father, who believed that the crucial trouble to resolving his diverse fitness troubles changed into bodily exertion. This changed into a few factor that appealed to Roosevelt. Indeed, this desire to enhance his physical stature was surely something that might pass straight away to preserve his existence in more strategies than one.

His father had extended held the perception
that this may be a way of helping his son
deal with his allergies. It is perception that
on nights wherein Roosevelt changed into
specially suffering that his father need to
take him out for a adventure in his carriage.
The idea became that the wind in his face
may efficiently strain air deep into his lungs,
permitting him to breathe more with out
problem.

In addition, his father moreover got here to
the perception that there might be some
factor incorrect with Roosevelt's eyesight
even as he observed that Roosevelt grow to
be no longer able to peer dreams that
considered one of a kind boys his age have
been capable of shoot with a few diploma of
accuracy. As a stop result, his father took
him for a watch constant take a look at, in
which it become decided that Roosevelt
modified into very near-sighted, main to
him being given glasses for the primary
time. This may, of path, circulate without

delay to come to be clearly his trademark, however being able to see the world this in fact turn out to be some factor that might in the long run change the life of Roosevelt. Indeed, it unfold out a current-day manner of seeing subjects, and it's miles absolutely feasible that this discovery connected to his eyesight certainly did form the relaxation of his existence.

We formerly said how his father encouraged him to get greater physical if you want to fight his bronchial allergies and it introduced about a gymnasium being set up inside the circle of relatives home. It want to be said that the opportunity kids inside the family moreover suffered from severa physical illnesses, so it modified into no longer genuinely for his own use. Roosevelt became then pressured into taking thing in a software program of every gymnastics and weight-lifting to help him bring together his body, due to the reality even his father stated, "You have the thoughts but you have not the body. You need to make the body." Roosevelt took this recommendation to coronary heart, most vital to him growing what need to satisfactory be defined as a rugged frame. Furthermore, he additionally developed a love for boxing, wrestling, and horse using, all sports sports that he ought to hold an interest in throughout his existence.

So, what are we capable to say approximately the early teenagers of Theodore Roosevelt? It emerge as not ugly in any way and he additionally have end up no longer required to put up with numerous hardships which might be regularly related to exclusive presidents.

Chapter 12: His Education

We said inside the first financial disaster how Roosevelt became informed at domestic because of his health problems, however this end up the equal for all the youngsters of the Roosevelt family. It is perception that that that they had tutors, their aunt, Anna Bulloch, further to a French governess. Their mom moreover took an energetic feature in their early training, but as they advanced and moved nearer closer to the idea of going to university, it is believed that she took extra of a records feature, and in reality ensured that their youngsters were really receiving the shape of tutoring that they required.

Considering he become informed certainly at home, it modified into an achievement to then be admitted to the outstanding Harvard University in 1876. During his time there, he studied diverse subjects along with zoology, German, natural records, composition, and additionally forensics.

However, none of those topics would possibly flow immediately to have any actual function in his lifestyles aside from, in all likelihood, his choice to look at extra approximately natural information, because an critical issue of his Presidency have become the selection to defend herbal resources in the course of the united states.

We are nevertheless used to Harvard being appeared as an area of check for the elite and this become nonetheless the have an effect on given with the resource of the university at the time Roosevelt attended. Indeed, it end up visible via many as being now not some thing more than only a finishing college for the rich, to shine their abilities preceding to them getting into both organization, law, or politics. Going to Harvard ought to come up with an advantage in lifestyles on the equal time as you left there, but for Roosevelt it have become extra approximately the studying aspect.

Harvard University at that point became no longer visible inside the maximum favorable mild. Indeed, in 1876, Horace E. Scudder wrote a bit of writing in Scribner's Monthly in which he voiced his rather dim opinion on what modified into happening inside the ones hallowed corridors.

"That repression or maybe disdain of enthusiasm, that emulation of immoderate-bred cynicism and conceited coolness, which in a more youthful man do now not be-token the healthiest, most effective man or woman, is normal. The diving fervor of enthusiasm is brazenly, or thru implication, voted a vulgar thing."

This have become the surroundings that the young Roosevelt is probably released into some 3 months after the difficulty grow to be published. However, from what we realize approximately his time at Harvard, Roosevelt was doing what he should to struggle decrease back in competition to the perceived stereotype of its students.

His severa contemporaries had been especially on the top of society in and round Boston. However, as we've were given seen inside the quote from Scudder, the way wherein they behaved themselves or approached their research changed into wonderful from Roosevelt, even though that isn't to say that he emerge as now not inspired through those spherical him. In real fact, it's far not unusual through way of numerous scholars that his thoughts surrounding the concept of each elegance or even recognition in society had been in huge issue usual with the aid of his time at Harvard.[2]

Most of the students which have been attending Harvard have been aware of the truth that their destiny had specifically been mapped out for them already. This delivered about them clearly no longer taking their research as substantially as they need to have, no matter the fact that the equal couldn't be said for Roosevelt. For him, it turn out to be about furthering his education. But the equal couldn't be said for max of his classmates. Instead, they saw this as a time to party. It is time-honored that Roosevelt felt precise disdain for the ones university university college students that noticed in shape to attend brothels and really reputation on socializing in desire to improving themselves.

It is for that very motive that we see Roosevelt gravitating a ways from his fellow college college students and spending greater time alongside collectively along with his lecturers, with whom he felt that he ought to analyze greater.

A amount of his classmates, who have been later quoted regarding their studies with the more youthful Roosevelt, commented at the way in which he speedy have become stated for his enthusiasm and the strength with which he may additionally input discussions and honestly take maintain of the whole state of affairs. To many, his electricity have become limitless, a pleasing that might serve him well at some point of his lifestyles, even though it modified into regularly seen as being quite unfavourable whilst he end up more younger.

However, in a sign that this changed into now not the regular manner of drawing near discussions, it's miles as an alternative thrilling to be aware that a number of his classmates had been cited to have placed his approach as being as an opportunity disconcerting and offensive. Furthermore, severa colleagues furthermore appeared his enthusiasm in discussions or arguments are being a supply of embarrassment, due to him in reality being no longer capable of manage his ardour.

To simply show the way that a number of human beings felt about his technique, we are capable of are seeking advice from an incident defined with the useful resource of a current of his time at Harvard, Bradley Gilman who found Roosevelt having a dialogue with beginners inside the corridors.[3]

"I modified into struck with the resource of way of the earnestness with which he become putting forth some thing to the opposite . He emphasized his factors thru complete of existence actions of the top, and through putting his right first into his left palm."

This is a effective picture. This have come to be an character that become forthright in his opinion and no longer afraid to talk his mind. It is probably no surprise for us to then discover that some of fellow students at Harvard might exit in their way to avoid entering a communicate or debate with Roosevelt in fact because of his overpowering nature.

Further evidence of his nature, and in reality his character, are even obvious in the way wherein he would possibly cope with human beings from far away. It turn out to be now not regarded as being the completed detail to shout across a courtyard in order to draw interest to yourself, however that changed into not a few aspect that regarded to be of assignment to Roosevelt. The Rev. Sherrard Billings commented on how even his tempo of movement have become an problem at Harvard.

"When it grow to be now not considered correct form to transport at greater than a stroll, Roosevelt became typically taking walks."

We said in advance how Harvard come to be appeared as being the final issue whereby those from an elite facts have to socialize and song the talents that could permit them to guide a rich existence, but that have emerge as a few component that modified into of grave subject to Roosevelt. He had been taught that those from this form of records have to correctly exit of their manner to offer lower returned to their community and to help parents who have been no longer as fortunate. This was some aspect that stuck with Roosevelt. It introduced on him feeling a advantageous degree of disgust at what he considered as an abuse of their elite function via so a whole lot of his contemporaries.

The trouble for Roosevelt modified into his incapacity to maintain the ones reviews to himself, which brought about a number of discussions and arguments with those classmates that he felt have been taking advantage in their state of affairs. It is likewise felt through many who his time at Harvard clearly customary the idea for the placement he might also undertake in his political career in opposition to the ones in America that held masses strength thanks to their wealth.

Athletics at Harvard

However, his time at Harvard modified into no longer all disappointing to Roosevelt, as he excelled at every his studies further to athletics.

He had already hung out operating on his power and fitness for a number of years previous to his arrival at Harvard, and he quick decided diverse sports activities activities clubs that allowed him to indulge in his diverse passions whilst now not interfering alongside collectively with his studies. Ideally, he can also have loved playing either soccer or baseball for the college, however troubles together along with his eyesight meant that this changed into now not feasible. Indeed, he failed to in reality take part in any organized sports activities sports, despite the fact that he modified into able to maintain along with his physical games.

Furthermore, we recognize that he did spend an low priced amount of time inside the health club and participated in boxing on a number of events. However, the bloodless wintry weather months may want to normally cause severa troubles together with his hypersensitive reactions, forcing him to significantly lessen time spent going for walks out.

It is also believed that his involvement in athletics allowed him to in the end get in the course of as a minimum a number of his classmates. Indeed, he would possibly pass directly to set up a number of critical relationships with severa individuals who can also want to themselves pass at once to have wonderful careers.

Studies at Harvard

When it got here to his research, then there can be no question that Roosevelt excelled at Harvard. Indeed, he's often quoted as having often challenged his professors on quite a number of factors, such became his self notion. This argumentative approach was something that might in the end end up a cornerstone of his method to politics, no matter the truth that that would be in a barely more delicate manner than the strategies he employed in the path of his time at Harvard.

To a few, his penchant for tackling his professors stemmed from his previous training having come from personal tutors. He have become used to being capable of venture them, and he surely took that approach with him to Harvard, even though it end up unique to how the majority of humans noticed their instructions at the university. His professors themselves ought to were taken aback by manner of this technique as he become as an alternative forceful in his desires that they answer his problems and questions.

As a student, he changed into not great in each state of affairs, with the aid of any way. However, he become difficult-working and diligent, and there can be no question that he did outperform some of his contemporaries. Of path, he would possibly then pass directly to surpass all of them with what he grow to be able to benefit afterward in existence.

It is notion that Roosevelt lengthy had to emerge as a scientist, however alas for him, one in every of his poorest topics become arithmetic, and this brought approximately him efficiently being forced proper proper into a profession in both politics or law. As it grew to turn out to be out, he may incorporate himself in every in some unspecified time in the future of his existence.

That is not to say that he absolutely gave up on his love of technology. Indeed, throughout his lifestyles, he may want to move back to the barren region and write books on topics related to nature. His love for it have grow to be apparent to all. However, he modified into no longer capable of make any development on this location throughout his time at Harvard, some component that is cited to have disappointed him a high-quality deal.

By the time he have grow to be coming to the give up of his time at Harvard, the younger Roosevelt needed to cautiously don't forget the route wherein he preferred his existence to transport. After lots concept, he came to the belief that strolling in regulation would have to suffice.

So what are we able to find out approximately the schooling of Roosevelt and the way it shaped him as an person? It suggests us how his particular fashion of politics and tackling the troubles of the day have been inspired through his education. Having recognize for the ones in positions of power did now not advise he could now not assignment them to offer an cause in their position, or difficulty out that they have got been incorrect.

Chapter 13: His Early Career

After graduating from Harvard, Roosevelt believed that his future lay in regulation and, as a end result, he entered Columbia Law School. However, this became part of his lifestyles that would not exercise quite as he predicted it to. It ended with him ultimately losing out of college earlier than he come to be capable of graduate. It is important to thing out that there have been some quite accurate reasons as to why he dropped out that we are capable of cowl later, however he end up already turning into upset with the concept of running in regulation prior to this happening.

For a number of motives, this a part of his existence is a few aspect that is often speedy glossed over while in real truth it tells us quite a variety of of factors about no longer simplest him as a person, but furthermore how he changed into typically aware of what he want to do together collectively with his lifestyles at any given time. It additionally shows how he became the shape of character who become quite glad to confess when they had made the wrong choice and then take steps to rectify matters as quick as viable.

It is truthful to say that Roosevelt did now not exactly set the sector on hearth for the duration of his time at regulation school, but he emerge as nevertheless responsible of arguing his critiques at any given possibility, which makes it alternatively weird that he did not sincere properly as a lawyer. It is bizarre to expect that we recognize little approximately his capability to argue topics from a felony mindset even as you don't forget how properly an orator he would emerge as.

Those which have studied the lifestyles of Roosevelt have commonly come to the realization that his desire to attend regulation school have become not out of a few absolute desire to turn out to be a attorney. Instead, it is assumed that he came to the realization that he had to have some form of career and he became not too concerned approximately the law. He did no longer show the equal kind of enthusiasm for his time at regulation university as he did both together along with his personal tutors or at Harvard. There are numerous motives why this may be the case.

The hassle for him, if it could be judged as such, changed into that even Roosevelt himself understood that there has been no real want for him to visit every other university as he didn't ought to work on the way to survive. For him, lifestyles have become a bit less difficult than that, as even Roosevelt himself have become quoted as saying:

"I had sufficient to get bread. What I had to do, if I preferred butter and jam, changed into to provide the butter and jam, however to take into account their price in comparison with numerous things. In one of a kind terms, I made up my mind that, on the identical time as I should earn cash, I should manipulate to pay for to make creating a living the secondary in area of the number one object of my career."[4]

It is apparent that Roosevelt have turn out to be able to genuinely loosen up if he desired to perform that, however the hassle for him have end up that his own family had a piece ethic that did now not allow this. To his family, he had to expose that he became running on some component.

The Roosevelt own family had lengthy felt the want to try to fulfill what they saw as their social obligations, as they got here from a privileged heritage. They had to show that they were inclined to help those in greater want. This turn out to be also some issue that Roosevelt agreed with, so that would have been part of his reasoning as to why regulation became the avenue that he had decided to transport down.

For a few, the first-class attraction that there could have been for Roosevelt in regulation modified into that he need to argue that the money end up surely of secondary importance. For him, know-how after which prevailing the cases might be seen as greater vital. Making a difference inside the lives of the humans he have turn out to be representing allowed him to meet his social responsibilities on the equal time. He by no means regarded upon the organisation as one that could make him fabulously wealthy.

Having his Eyes Opened to the Law

Roosevelt entered regulation university with a few very set mind as to what the regulation changed into like and the way it helped human beings in want, but he as an alternative quickly determined that this changed into now not precisely the case. Instead, he began to revel in as an opportunity despondent that the large and effective man or woman within the case, irrespective of if it turn out to be plaintiff or defendant, should pop out on pinnacle in greater instances than no longer. At this point, he felt that the law turn out to be possibly no longer as correct as he concept.

This problem of factors not being socially honest have become some component that would maintain cropping up in his existence and truly, it'd shape a key part of his development as a baby-kisser. To Roosevelt, it was not possible for there to be a 'sincere deal' which have grow to be a term that as we are able to see might waft directly to become as an alternative essential for him throughout his time as President.

Roosevelt and Thinking About Politics

It turn out to be inside the direction of his time at regulation college that Roosevelt started to simply take extra of an interest in politics and attended some political conferences. Considering the way in which he have grow to be viewing the law, it's far no wonder that he felt that the nice humans that had been able to address what he noticed as being social injustice have been politicians. It is probably argued that it grow to be at this second that he determined that a flow into from the regulation into the arena of politics might be exceptional for him. It may pass right now to become the superb decision that he may ever make in his lifestyles.

Throughout a as a substitute quick time period, Roosevelt started to be drawn similarly into the political worldwide. In the manner, it have become turning into more and more apparent to him that the attraction of regulation modified into diminishing. He changed into becoming stuck up within the manner wherein politics were in a position to influence numerous elements of existence, as opposed to him searching for to consciousness on one region. Roosevelt understood that politicians might artwork at the legal guidelines, the monetary device, conservation, civil rights, and a lot more.

At the same time, his disillusionment with the regulation have become moreover becoming far extra obvious. He become of the opinion that it changed into surely incapable of ruling in a trustworthy way. He had specific problems with the legal tips that handled the connection among provider and client. In his opinion, the regulation need to have made advantageous that every facets were capable of advantage, however his information of the regulation led him to the notion that it might nearly usually thing with the seller.

To Roosevelt, this emerge as very incorrect on some of ranges and he commenced out to in reality revel in that it turned into now not possible for him to keep on in a profession that became going immediately in competition to his personal private ideals and philosophy. The entire technique became so taxing on his thoughts and morals that he felt compelled to leave the career earlier than he changed into genuinely capable of correctly begin. Indeed, for masses, this have become a easy early signal of the manner Roosevelt ought to constantly are looking for for to take the ethical stance.

Ultimately, Theodore Roosevelt decided to head away law university in 1881 and it modified into not as even though he had a hard and fast plan in region, each. You have to bear in mind that he had already stated that developing a living end up a secondary detail and that it modified into extra to do with locating a career that could make a difference to society and people in desired. If walking within the law emerge as not the profession for him, then it might not go away too many special alternatives even though it modified into turning into clean to Roosevelt that the area of politics might be higher relevant as his calling.

We stated how he had commenced to attend political meetings throughout his time at law college. However, his idea of getting into this notoriously difficult international while no longer having any form of career to fall lower again on turn out to be specific and showed that he modified into each rather assured in his potential or that he come to be identifying to stick strongly to his principles of pleasant performing some problem wherein he ought to help human beings.

However, his time as a flesh presser might be included in a series of highs and lows, with elections received and misplaced as well as lacking out on key nominations due to his particular style and his refusal to back off from a combat.

So, how are we able to summarize his early career? Well, if we are being honest about it, then we must come to the notion that he correctly did not have one, because of dropping out from regulation college early.

It is tough for us to return to any sort of a conclusion as to what his destiny could have been had he no longer lengthy long gone to regulation faculty, as it end up there that he began out to revel in the draw of politics and attended his first political meetings. How some distance he predicted to transport within the global of politics is up for debate.

Chapter 14: His Developing Family Life

Clearly the circle of relatives lifestyles of Roosevelt changed into something that would broaden in the course of his lifetime, however we can address his non-public existence within the one bankruptcy for ease of reading.

Theodore Roosevelt have grow to be a sturdy own family guy. This modified into some element that is diagnosed approximately him even from his days as a toddler. He idolized his father and at the same time loved his mom or even after their respective deaths he made certain that he remained in near contact together with his siblings at some point of his life. To him, they original an essential a part of who he changed into and the way he were lengthy-hooked up as a baby and this modified into some issue that he took with him while he commenced to check developing his very circle of relatives.

The first 2nd in his life that we need to point out changed into his very first marriage on the age of 22 to a first-rate socialite of the time, Alice Hathaway Lee. She modified into the daughter of a first rate banker. They had a daughter in 1884 thru the decision of Alice Lee Roosevelt. However, the pleasure could be very short-lived for the own family, with the partner of Roosevelt loss of life in reality days after the delivery of their toddler, from what have emerge as defined as a kidney problem.

This devastated Roosevelt, as now he modified into with out a wife and but had a totally younger infant to keep up. This modified into no longer the most effective lack of life that he had to address at that aspect; in a cruel twist of future his cherished mom, Mittie, had died of typhoid fever within the actual same house exceptional 11 hours earlier.

Due to this double hit, it's miles possibly no wonder that he at the start decided to depart his daughter inside the custody of his sister whilst he went thru the grieving manner. However, he can also count on custody of her all all over again by the point she grow to be 3 years antique. In the intervening time, he took time in an effort to try to heal. He have been very close to his mom, and of path to his more youthful spouse; it might were a hard double blow for everyone to take. The very fact that he have become able to no longer simplest come again from it, however accomplish that in a thoughts-blowing manner, tells you loads approximately the person of the person.

It is apparent that the dying of Alice hit Roosevelt tough. Indeed, in his diary he's recognized to have sincerely marked the date with an X and stated that the mild had prolonged long past out of his lifestyles. He need to not often write approximately her at some point of the rest of his lifestyles.

The grieving technique changed into interrupted through Edith Kermit Carow. Edith should cross directly to no longer handiest grow to be the affection of his existence, but his associate till his death days.

Edith changed into from time to time unknown to Roosevelt, as she had grown up beside him as a little one. She changed into additionally the extremely good pal of Roosevelt's more youthful sister, Corinne. It is also commonly famous that she have become the number one person out of doors of his proper now family that Roosevelt truely finished with. The two must play inside the identical kindergarten as children. Indeed, it's also advocated that the mother of Roosevelt felt that there was a few form of friendship developing between the 2, even though definitely it became not viable to expect that things might increase to this amount in a while in life.

Furthermore, it's far believed with the aid of the usage of way of a few that the two of them developed a few type of dating as teens, so that they have got been romantically worried to a sure quantity, however this romance got here to an cease with out every body actually being aware. However, it is believed that it turned into not extended after the end of this romance that Roosevelt commenced out to try to woo Alice Lee. Edith is probably present at their bridal ceremony now not lengthy after he graduated from university.

However, after the premature death of Alice in 1884, Edith all over again became crucial inside the existence of Roosevelt, rekindling their relationship in 1885. The courting is understood to have commenced in advance than it have become introduced to the public, as Roosevelt become of the opinion that, as he turned into although getting over the loss of life of his first partner, that it might be too quickly for him to show that he changed into in some different dating. They were ultimately married in London on December 2d 1886.

The couple then launched into a 15 week honeymoon tour of Europe, in advance than returning to the United States to allow Roosevelt to preserve alongside with his profession. Upon returning, the couple moved into the residence on Long Island close to Oyster Bay that he had initially started out out to construct for his first associate. However, he did change the call of the house from LeeHolm to Sagamore Hill. This domestic may want to in the end come to be their favored place to retreat to, even if Roosevelt become inside the White House. After his demise it'd additionally emerge as the region where Edith have to stay for the rest of her living days.

After his marriage to Edith, he sought to regain custody of his daughter from his first marriage. He felt that they had been now a strong sufficient circle of relatives, and he had recovered from his preliminary loss sufficiently, to offer her with the upbringing that she deserved. Edith and himself must pass immediately to have a complete of five youngsters with 4 sons and one daughter, with Edith additionally having at least one miscarriage that we're aware of.

The thrilling issue approximately this circle of relatives is that the American people really took to them, especially at some stage in the years inside the White House. They have been the number one instance of America falling in love with the First Family, some problem that has carried on because then. Indeed, the media of the time need to frequently report and touch upon troubles concerning the family, so that you can see how it is perhaps a precursor to what has long past on due to the truth.

It isn't always any marvel that there are a number of photographs of the family at the White House, as they were vital celebrities at a time in which the concept of the movie celeb did not pretty exist inside the manner we're acquainted with these days.

Moving Around the Country

Even despite the fact that the Roosevelts did have their domestic on Long Island to move decrease returned to, lifestyles as a baby-kisser concerned transferring round some of times. This have become the case with Theodore Roosevelt, but his spouse and kids have been extraordinary too happy to comply with in form so that it will useful aid him and additionally hold the family unit together.

However, by the point Roosevelt have end up President and moved into the White House, the own family had already lived in Washington D.C. On two special activities. They to begin with lived inside the Washington place among 1889 and 1895, whilst Roosevelt worked because the chairman for the us Civil Service Commission. They had been then compelled into moving again to Washington absolutely two years later, in 1897 till 1898, even as Roosevelt emerge as the assistant secretary for the navy. This fairly happy his partner and changed into rather critical for Roosevelt.

Aside from living in Washington, in addition they had to skip back in the direction of their roots in 1899, on the equal time as Roosevelt have emerge as the governor of New York. However, this will high-quality final for some distinct years, earlier than the circle of relatives have become pressured into moving lower lower back to Washington D.C for a 3rd time (regardless of the truth that this have end up to stay within the White House, which emerge as a very excellent proposition for them.)

As a instead thrilling apart, presidents because of the reality Roosevelt can thank his spouse for their having more place in the White House. It turn out to be established via individuals who had come before him that topics have been barely cramped inside the building and that it end up no longer honestly that appropriate for the number one family to stay in. However, even as the Roosevelt own family moved in, that they had some of youngsters to attend to, further to numerous body of workers and protection, and it became truly no longer feasible for them to live there because it emerge as.

As a end quit end result, Edith Roosevelt set approximately converting subjects within the White House. She have become the number one instigator behind the improvement of the West Wing, which is probably used to house all the brilliant Presidential places of work. Up until this element, those workplaces had been stuffed in beside the dwelling area for the family, which modified into infrequently an excellent answer. Indeed, it need to also be said that although it turn out to be often called the White House, that did no longer emerge as its right name till Theodore Roosevelt made it so.

His Relationship with His Family

There isn't any doubt that Roosevelt loved being the President, however he come to be clearly prouder of being a father and took brilliant pride in seeing his children develop and make bigger for the duration of their lives. This feeling inside the direction of his family became some thing that have become effectively obvious and it contributed to the way wherein they have been appeared in society.

Indeed, we're able to in reality get a glimpse into the manner in which he taken into consideration his own family in a letter that he wrote to his 15 12 months vintage son, Kermit upon his re-election in 1904.

"No be counted how matters came out, the genuinely important detail became the cute existence with Mother and you children, and that in comparison to this home existence the whole lot else emerge as of small significance from the perspective of happiness."[5]

As we are able to see from this quote, it's miles clean that he changed into pretty content cloth fabric to location family in advance than a few trouble else, even a characteristic as effective as President, and this idea may be harassed even in addition through another quote:

"There isn't always any form of happiness at the Earth, no shape of any fulfillment of any kind, that during any way tactics the happiness of the husband and the partner who are married fanatics, and the moms and dads of masses of healthful kids."[6]

The problem for Roosevelt have grow to be that there had been a number of times at some stage in the early lives of his children that he become pressured to be a protracted way from them. This modified into troubling to him, as he struggled with being away from those he cherished the most. Ultimately, it'd bring about Roosevelt writing them a chain of letters, so as to show that they have been nevertheless utmost in his mind. These letters may additionally then shape a ebook, Theodore Roosevelt's Letters to his Children, which have end up published throughout the time of his death and feature emerge as a large hit. Indeed, this e book wonderful similarly cemented the recognition and emotions of appreciation inside the route of the own family which have been with them at some point in their time in the White House.

His circle of relatives emerge as capable of affecting him in methods that nothing else have to. Indeed, he changed into brief to announce while he changed into satisfied with their achievements in life, and it's also acknowledged that the loss of lifestyles of his son in World War I despatched him spinning proper right into a deep despair from which he in no way clearly recovered to any excellent extent. Aside from that one problem, his own family life have become satisfied, and he have become extra than content to interrupt out from the arena of politics and spend time with the ones he cherished the most.

Chapter 15: His Introduction Into Politics

When it includes his introduction to politics, we must go again slightly in time to even as he end up a student at Harvard, as the roots of some of his ideals were extra than probable fashioned within the direction of this period of his life.

During his first few years on the university, Roosevelt's father had end up greater interested in, now not wonderful politics, but the idea of political reform. He is understood to have taken pretty a company stance inside the route of what he noticed due to the fact the Republican device in and spherical New York State, and he made some in-roads in his early political career.

Indeed, such turned into his success as an propose for political reform, that it delivered approximately President Hayes electing Roosevelt Senior to the location of federal tariff collector for New York.

This changed into a function that held a few prominence, however he turn out to be not completed there collectively with his ability political profession. The flow via manner of Hayes to appoint Roosevelt senior to this characteristic was a clear strive at seeking to fight decrease back toward those he noticed as having an excessive amount of political power. He end up conscious that Roosevelt senior might no longer stand for insolence and corruption.

However, there was a hassle. There were enough human beings in the Republican celebration, which includes Senator Roscoe Conkling, that when the appointment of Roosevelt senior have become placed to Congress, the flow into turn out to be defeated 31 votes to twenty-5.

This is the instant regarded with the useful resource of many as being a key point in the political thoughts of Roosevelt. To him, the fact that a handful of effective people come to be capable of block reforms that he saw as being essential modified into indicative of methods corrupt politics were, particularly inside the Republican Party. This unsettled him to such an amount that he there and then determined that some thing ought to must take region to the manner wherein businesses and nice key people were able to paintings towards justice. To Roosevelt, it end up clean that the welfare of the humans in elegant become the most important trouble, and some problem that were given in the manner had to be dealt with therefore. It modified into an hassle that he may deal with time and time yet again by the time he have been given to the White House.

It is tough to us of a that if his father were dealt with better then possibly Roosevelt would possibly have mellowed slightly in his method to the problem of corruption. However, that have become now not the case, and Roosevelt must make an entire career out of the concept of taking the ones individuals and companies to challenge for his or her unlawful and unfair techniques of doing topics.

Getting Started in Politics

In order to chart the political development of Roosevelt, we need to transport decrease decrease lower back to 1882 and his election to the New York State Assembly, as this come to be the number one time he made it publicly recounted that he changed into interested in growing a career in politics. By this time, Roosevelt had already standard some of his key thoughts. His choice to get into close by politics have become being pushed by the usage of his choice to right what he discovered as a number of wrongs, or even a number of crimes, in competition to no longer excellent the u . S . But the usual public.

At this factor in information, the complete local political scene emerge as now not for the faint-hearted. It emerge as a difficult area to characteristic, with such a lot of humans determined to further their personal purpose, or being open to corruption, that it have turn out to be hard for an person to definitely strike out on their private. This have turn out to be specifically real in and round New York, in which matters had been more difficult than in most locations. Roosevelt modified into now not remove via this prospect and as a substitute threw himself into it from the outset.

However, the best hassle that Roosevelt confronted became that he grow to be in big element restricted in the political birthday party that he may also need to certainly have a examine. He grow to be appeared as being an aristocrat and for a number of human beings there has been the opinion that the Democrats have been slightly rougher and more tough in their technique to existence. This have come to be then visible as not being an high-quality suit for his upbringing despite the fact that it can be argued that some of his policies and political opinions were aligned more toward the Democrats. It positioned him in a quite unique function despite the reality that Roosevelt made it smooth that he have become his private man and couldn't be prompted via way of what he end up anticipated to do through others.

It became now not all simple crusing for Roosevelt, as he made it clean that he intended to turn out to be involved inside the global of politics, and it have become his own buddies that have been the maximum important of his thoughts. However, it have to be referred to that maximum of his pals had been each legal professionals or operating in senior positions in banking, and to them the concept of being a flesh presser became a few issue that changed into truly no longer suitable sufficient. In distinct phrases, there was a hint of snobbery approximately their approach to existence and as a stop end result they have been responsible of scoffing on the mind held thru Roosevelt.

This opinion modified into then most effective able to reinforcing thoughts that Roosevelt already had regarding the effect that enterprise and the sector of finance had on politics. His friends were of the notion that they have been able to use their affect from their very very own unique worldwide a good way to efficiently make political trade. This emerge as some difficulty that had dissatisfied Roosevelt for some time, as he had already placed how employer and powerful human beings had controlled to have a horrific impact on the capability destiny profession of his very personal father.

Developing his Career as a Politician

Even despite the fact that his buddies were actually in competition to his concept of becoming a flesh presser, it turn out to be not a few issue that he may also want to permit to unduly have an impact on him. Instead, Roosevelt's mind on a way to development as a flesh presser were as an alternative terrific, as he understood that it become crucial for him to stay near to the ones who've been regarded as being influential at the smaller, neighborhood level. This in itself emerge as a smart approach to take, considering what have become at stake, and this capability to select out the right human beings to intention emerge as a few element that he could keep to take advantage of ultimately of his career.

www.ingramcontent.com/pod-product-compliance
Lightning Source LLC
Chambersburg PA
CBHW061507050726
47593CB00002B/487

* 9 7 8 1 7 7 5 3 1 4 2 9 5 *